In the still semi-darkness a great yearning overwhelms me.
I feel the weight of all the memories and all the longing.

 g in the silence and an immutable
he stillness. I slip out of bed and
shoulders to keep out the chill of
up at me through the glimmer, his
e all dark and deep in the absence
of light.

I lean in towards him and take his face in my hands. For
. fragment of time, the knowledge that he is still here with
me is, inexplicably, almost enough. I search the familiar
corners of his face and look deep into the eyes that hold
nine. There is such a sense of wonder in that feeling as he
olds my gaze.

I reach down and close my hand around his, lifting the
alm away from the hard splint, tracing the shape of his
ngers, feeling their warmth. I let my head sink down
wards his onto the blank whiteness of the pillow. And for
moment, for a precious fleeting moment, we are at peace.

Hasso von Bredow was born in Germany in 1958. He met his wife, Catherine, in 1982 and came to live in the UK a few years later. After some years in Devon, he took up a successful banking career in the City. At the age of 42 he suffered a massive stroke at the base of his brainstem, which left him the victim of 'locked-in' syndrome. Totally paralysed but completely cognisant, Hasso was reduced to using coded blinking and state of the art technology to communicate with those around him. After a year in hospital, he was finally able to return home to Catherine and their three children. There, letter by letter, using a specially adapted computer, he completed the painstaking task of writing this incredibly moving memoir. Tragically, Hasso died of pneumonia in 2004.

Born in Devon in 1958, Catherine von Bredow became a teacher in the early '80s. When her husband, Hasso, was disabled by a massive stroke in 2000, Catherine left work and spent the next four years as Hasso's carer until his death in 2004. In the process of publishing Hasso's memoir, she was invited to contribute to his book by examining the impact his stroke had had on her own life and on the lives of their children. *In the Blink of an Eye* not only charts her experience of grief and the pain of witnessing Hasso's suffering; it also unfolds for the reader a tender and inspiring portrait of the extraordinary man she loved so much and whose loss changed her for ever. Catherine continues to live at the family home in Kent where she now devotes her time to writing.

In the Blink of an Eye

Hasso and Catherine von Bredow

An Orion paperback

First published in Great Britain in 2009
by Orion
This paperback edition published in 2010
by Orion Books Ltd,
Orion House, 5 Upper St Martin's Lane,
London WC2H 9EA

An Hachette UK company

1 3 5 7 9 10 8 6 4 2

A CIP catalogue record for this book is available
from the British Library.

ISBN 978-0-7528-8401-1

Printed and bound in Great Britain by Clays Ltd, St Ives plc

www.orionbooks.co.uk

This book is dedicated to my three wonderful children, Lucia, Sophia and Christian, who all had to learn the eye alphabet and helped their mummy to look after me at the drop of a hat. A classic case of role reversal.

Hasso

Acknowledgements

This book would never have been published without the intervention of certain key people. I would like to thank David Mackin at Greengate Publishing for his generous encouragement and support in the early days of this venture. My deep-felt thanks also to Lisa Milton and to the fantastic team at Orion for all their encouragement and nurturing. I am indebted in particular to my editors, Amanda Harris, who championed Hasso's book and encouraged me to write, and to Daniel Bunyard whose rare patience, kind coaxing and clear-sightedness were so crucial in helping me to knock our manuscripts into shape. I would also like to extend my thanks to Anna Carroll for her superb proofreading and to Christine King for her inspired help with the title.

To my agent and dear friend, Sheila Ableman, I owe an enormous debt of gratitude. She had the vision, courage and tenacity to fight for Hasso's story all the way and to enable me to release his voice to the world.

On Hasso's behalf, I want to take this opportunity to express profound and lasting gratitude to everyone, family, friends and carers, who played their part, however great or small, in loyally supporting him through all his locked-in years, in encouraging his efforts to write and in humanising his care with so much genuine love and kindness.

Finally, I would also like to thank my mother for her enduring strength and support and, in particular, for her patient reading of the manuscript. Above all, though, thanks are due to my three wonderful children, who have so much of Hasso in them, and without whom I certainly would not have come this far.

Catherine

Angfangs wollt'ich fast verzagen,
Und ich glaubt', ich trüg' es nie;
Und ich hab' es doch getragen —
Aber fragt mich nur nicht, wie?

At first I almost despaired,
And I thought I would never be able to bear it;
Yet even so, I have borne it —
But do not ask me how.

'Junge Leiden', Heinrich Heine, Lieder VII
(Translation Emily Ezust)

Locked-in syndrome: a rare neurological disorder characterised by complete paralysis of voluntary muscles in all parts of the body except for those that control eye movement. Individuals with locked-in syndrome are conscious and can think and reason, but are unable to speak or move. The disorder leaves individuals completely mute and paralysed. Communication may be possible with blinking eye movements.

There is no cure.

Source: National Institute of Neurological Disorders and Stroke

Preface

I was twenty-four when I came face to face with the young man who was to change my life forever. Tall, good-looking and blessed with a natural, easy charm, he was unlike anyone I had ever known before or since.

Hasso would never have considered himself to be in any way special. But everyone who knew him tended to disagree. He was born in Hannover in 1958 into an old German family from whom he learned integrity, a strong sense of identity and courage in adversity. Hasso's heritage taught him from an early age to expect nothing but to give his all to any situation.

He was for me an irresistible jumble of seeming contradictions. Despite a vein of sometimes stern discipline running through his nature, Hasso was warm, generous-spirited and above all funny. He loved to laugh and to make others laugh. With his impeccable manners and his noble bearing, there was an old-world charm about him that set him apart and sometimes belied his easy-going, fun-loving personality. He loved rock music and heavy metal, but would kiss a lady's hand on being introduced. He wore jeans and leather but was equally at home in a traditional green hunting jacket or a tailored suit. He had no money, but carried himself with a sense of history and honour. He loved nothing more than to work in his garden and walk the woodland paths with his children, yet also had a fondness for smoke-filled bars and all-night drinking sessions with friends. Hasso embraced all these baffling opposites with equal enthusiasm and natural joy, never feeling the slightest sense of conflict or contradiction.

When I met him in Germany in September 1982, he was an infectious blend of enthusiasm and idealism.

Within hours of meeting him I knew that I could never bear to be parted from him. It was an unbelievable moment. He told me that very day that he had made up his mind that we should be together for the rest of our lives. He was calm and very sure. 'Everything is perfectly clear,' he said. And so it was. He remained steadfast in what he wanted. Never wavering, ever.

1 May 2000 dawned like any other day. I was not to know, however, that it was to be the last day of life as we had known it. When that day came to a close, Hasso, just forty-two years of age, had suffered a rare and massive stroke in his brainstem. Without the advanced technology of resuscitation it would certainly have killed him. There had been no sign, no warning. The picture was grim. He was totally paralysed and was being kept alive on a ventilator. Apart from his eyes, which he could still open and close, nothing else in his body would obey his brain. This vibrant, funny, charming man was now immobile and incontinent, unable to speak, eat, drink or breathe properly. Yet, as if all that were not enough, his mind, his senses, his clarity of perception remained untouched. Immured within the tomb of his otherwise perfectly healthy body, he was acutely aware of what had happened and totally conscious of the horror of it all. The medical term is 'locked in'. He was, in effect, buried alive.

The consequences were shattering. His 'night of the soul' was long and dark. During the four years that followed, he travelled a spiritual and emotional path neither he, nor anyone else, could have thought possible.

Confined to a hospital bed and a wheelchair and now incapable of independent living, Hasso found himself face to face with a life as far removed from his own as it was humanly possible to imagine. After almost a year in hospital, and in spite of the fact that his condition had failed to improve significantly, we finally managed, against the odds, to get him home to live with us.

For me, the effects of Hasso's stroke had been immediately and profoundly devastating. As he struggled to define himself within the parameters of his new existence, despite all my intense desire to help, I was faced with the realisation that I could do absolutely nothing to take away his suffering. The truth was unavoidable from the beginning: nothing I could do would ever be enough. All my efforts seemed dwarfed by the immensity of his condition. There was no way on earth I could change anything, and the man who was all the world to me now remained trapped behind the impenetrable walls of this prison.

Inevitably, the effect of that first year and of his struggle to find a way forward left an indelible mark on him. With the power of speech continuing to evade him, he nevertheless burned with the desire to connect with his world, his family and his friends, as well as with a growing compulsion to tell the story of his experiences. He felt driven to express the magnitude of what had happened and also to communicate to a wider readership the realities of a life 'locked in'. Throughout the long days and nights of his confinement in hospital, he had planned and structured the ideas for this book in his head, storing up details and memories for the time when he could transform them into the first draft of a text.

He began with characteristic aplomb. To my astonishment, one evening, within days of returning home, he used eye blinks to spell out a string of words to me. Although I was accustomed to his using this method to express his needs and thoughts, I was at first baffled by their apparent irrelevance to the moment. It didn't take me long, though, to realise what he was doing. This, I saw suddenly, was the beginning of a narrative, a book. It was to become his way out of the circle of silence. His body had become his own prison, but his brain was intact and his spirit unbowed. Inside, though deeply scarred, he was still the same person and he was now determined to use this book to prove it. It was his way of releasing the voice which had been taken from him.

Technology was to prove his ally on this front. Though almost completely paralysed, with only a tiny residue of voluntary movement in his thumb and the ability to open and close his eyes, he 'wrote' this account of his stroke and its consequences from his wheelchair; at first dictating with eye blinks, and then with the aid of a specially designed computer and ultra-sensitive switch system. Given the profound level of his disability, the process of writing in this way was complex and grindingly slow. Each day he would insist on spending hours and hours seated in his wheelchair in front of the computer, trying to articulate his thoughts and transfer them onto the screen. Letter by letter, his often unreliable, flickering thumb movement would select options from the on-screen talking keyboard until words slowly formed, multiplied and transformed themselves at a snail's pace into whole sentences. Sometimes, several hours of gruellingly tedious work would result in one short paragraph of a few sentences, produced in a massive size 72 font to the unremittingly droning voice of the scanner. On other days he achieved a little more; and then, after a short break, he would want to press on and on until, day by day, the text slowly piled up in front of him. Although he could not focus his eyes well enough or move them across the screen to actually read properly what he had written, he plodded on, depending on memory and my re-reading to help him. The painfully slow nature of the whole thing was, doubtless, intensely frustrating. But so was absolutely everything else. Here, at least, was a kind of liberation. The effort filled what had otherwise become the wretched tedium of his new life and, though he frequently found it exhausting, it gave him, finally, a very real sense of control and self-expression. He had found a way of translating himself, of revealing to anyone who might still doubt it that, below the rigid, frozen surface of his locked-in body, there ran the same deep, fast-flowing current as ever before.

For the next 18 months or so he laboured on like this. He was genuinely moved when friends and family urged him to publish the book and was encouraged by their enthusiasm for the snippets of text he would show them in response to their curiosity. 'I'll need your help with this . . . big time,' he told me, knowing that my promise was a given. In the final stages of the writing, he began to think about presentation and about the whole process of organising and editing the text which he knew would need restructuring somewhat. Because of the constraints of the composition process, he had only been able to write in a linear fashion, with no means of going back over his text, of rereading or reworking his pages. He solved the problem by adding extra information to his first completed version and I then had to find appropriate sections in the text to slip them in. He also wrote up detailed instructions about how he wanted the text organised. Occasionally I offered some thoughts of my own. Sometimes he liked my suggestions, sometimes he didn't. And he wasn't tentative in showing his rejection or disapproval of my ideas! We often ran into disagreements about tiny details; but in the end, as I saw it, it was his book and even if he knew I wasn't always quite comfortable with the way he wanted to present some of it, he also knew that I wouldn't interfere too much with the final version. Apart from some minor changes to structure and content, it was my primary concern to preserve his account in its entirety and to retain its authenticity. Over time, his growing tendency to compress and condense his sentences (in order, I suspect, to get to the end before his strength failed him) relied on my ability to decode or interpret them. This necessitated some expansion on my behalf and I used much of the 'extra information' pieces he wrote after he had finished the text proper, to flesh out these sections, always trying to preserve his words and fit them into the main body of the text.

Bouts of illness and discomfort frequently interrupted this process. We were often thrown off course by lack of time on my part (the demands of 24-hour care allow for few opportunities for proofreading and editing), and by exhaustion and frequently overwhelming periods of weakness or even depression on his. But he would always rally himself and focus his spirit one more time to the task in hand. Once he felt that the main part of the writing was complete, he would nevertheless frequently return to it, making new suggestions or writing additional material. Many of these were fascinating and full of interesting detail.

When I read the dedication, I understood not only how important the book itself was to him as a means of communicating the unimaginable, but how deeply he felt the compulsion to write and, by so doing, to give the children something of himself.

After his death, it took me a long, long time to find the courage to take up where he had so prematurely had to leave off. Regular enquiries about the book often left me feeling disappointed in myself and embarrassed at my inability to see it through. I felt unequal to the task and Hasso's dream of publication for a while remained just that. After almost two years, however, I finally found the resolve to return to the words he had so painstakingly created and to attempt to produce a manuscript that I could present for inspection.

Several months later, a friend recommended an agent who might be interested and, with much trepidation, I sent off the finished version for the first time. When asked to a meeting, I found the discussion about Hasso's condition and his writing really difficult and the subsequent kind but definitive refusal left me deflated. I wanted to give up. However, I decided that I would try to raise the cash myself to get the book published privately. That way, at least family and friends would be able to read it. The chance discovery of a publisher in our local area brought me in touch with the team who oversaw this first stage of the project to fruition. I could not have been more fortunate. The understanding and support they gave me resulted in 200 bound and printed copies of Hasso's manuscript, produced to the best standards within the most affordable format. I packaged these up and sent them out across the country and throughout the world to all of Hasso's family, friends and colleagues and to those who had been touched by him. And there, I thought, it had ended.

What followed, however, was both a surprise and a spur to action. Letters came pouring in from all those who had received it and from complete strangers to whom it had been passed on. I found their words deeply moving. All were, as one friend put it, 'profoundly affected'. Some, who had known and loved him before the stroke, mentioned how 'poignant and unforgettable' they found the characteristic humour and honesty of his words and that they would treasure them, almost as a kind of parting gift from him. Others, who had only got close to him in his 'locked-in' state, mentioned his courage and warmth and the regret that they had not had the chance to get to know him before. 'It is an extraordinary story told by someone whose strength of personality, bravery and compassion shines through on every page,' wrote someone whom I had never met, but who had been moved enough to write. Each letter expressed the conviction that Hasso's account should be more widely read and that his story was far too remarkable to be forgotten. Some medical professionals even wrote asking for ways of obtaining more copies, as they wanted to be able to recommend it to their students, to nurses and fellow doctors. 'There are many lessons in your book for doctors and nurses – in fact for all of us,' wrote one specialist. Again and again, people urged me to find a way to get it published properly so that it might, as one dear friend wrote, stand as a 'monument to the very best that is human', and a 'tribute to his spirit'.

I was overwhelmed. But there was something more. An immense pride welled up in me for the effect that Hasso's courage had had on others and how his efforts to break out of the prison of silence that engulfed him had transformed themselves into a life-changing, even a life-affirming force. He had shown unbelievable determination to make it happen. I knew that I couldn't now give up until the book had found its way towards publication and that I would have to devote myself with renewed vigour to making that happen.

In the event, it was Hasso's own words that pulled it off, firstly through the sensitive reception they received from the woman who would become our agent, Sheila Ableman, and then through the response and the inspired guidance of the team at Orion. Hesitatingly and, it has to be said, reluctantly, I now turned myself to the task they requested of me: that of writing about the experience from my own perspective. To this end, I was prompted and encouraged to revisit the journals I had written at the time and then to join my own voice to Hasso's by contributing to the final text. In the end, though I found the task daunting and, at times, all too emotionally draining, eventually I managed to find some way into unlocking a past that had been so unbearable. It may even be true that, by shining a light onto my own experience of Hasso's suffering, perhaps I discovered a path towards retrieving from the overwhelming sense of loss I felt a more complete picture of what he had gone through, of our life together and of what he meant to me. My emotions and my memories became a kind of language of their own, a way into expressing the inexpressible; a kind of journey, I suppose, both backwards and forwards. And always, at the front of my mind, stood the conviction that, if, by publishing this book, Hasso would, finally, really be able to tell it how it was, then that, for me, was worth the struggle. And I would have kept my promise.

In the end, this little book has become something momentous. For Hasso, it was a reassertion of his sense of self. Its voice is resolute and so recognisably his own. For all of us who loved him, it will remain a testament to his spirit and his courage.

Catherine, January 2009

PART ONE

From the Fast to the Slow Lane

May 2000

1 May 2000

There is a before and there is an after. There is a day, a moment when, abruptly, one life ends and another begins. When, without one even realising what is going on, life has become 'other'. A watershed.

You don't realise it at first. You can't even recognise that it has come. Your connection to your own self and to your life is so strong that you cannot contemplate the split. A seismic rift that has ripped life in two. Your brain needs time to catch up with the inexorable flow of the change. When it does, your life has already drifted off beyond your reach and the doors have slammed shut on what you believed yourself to be. In the blink of an eye, you are where you never desired yourself to be, a person unrecognisable to yourself, transformed beyond your own understanding. The before and the after. With no going back.

I lay prone in an ambulance. Outside, the world flew past me. May morning sunlight, now beyond my reach, birds traversing the sky on the upward lift of warm air, blossom and tender green leaves brushing the sides of the vehicle as it sped through the country lanes. Urgency imprinted itself on the landscape and on the buildings, darkly glimpsed through the tinted windows, as the blue light and sirens urged motorists and shoppers out of the way in the streets approaching the hospital.

Unprepared and unwilling as I was, I found myself propelled headlong towards the future prepared for me in the silence of time, come like a thief in the night to strip me of myself.

'I am only forty-two,' I thought. 'My God, I'm only forty-two.'

Blankness and gravity were etched on the faces around me. Outside, the world, my world, flew past with horrifying speed, past all those ordinary people who remained oblivious to the enormity of what was unfolding in my life.

'Oh, my God, I'm only forty-two.'

The words repeated themselves in my head like a mantra.

There was no reply.

It all began with the dawn of what promised to be a perfect day. I remember feeling all the impatience and excitement of waking to the beckoning sunshine of that warm May bank holiday morning and the children's delight at my suggestion of an early bike ride through the country lanes.

The night before, having completed many hours work on my laptop, I had gone to bed quite late. I was on my own in the house looking after the children, while my wife, Catherine, was visiting her family in Devon. We normally did everything like that together as a family, but this once had decided that Catherine should go alone for the weekend. Our eldest daughter, Lucia, was spending the night with a friend in the next village. So, taking advantage of the relative quiet, once the two younger ones had gone to bed, I had decided to give the household accounts a long-needed facelift. I had managed to amass a backlog of months of paperwork, and spent the whole evening sorting through it, recording individual notes in pencil against each item. These records were part of my own idiosyncratic system, developed over many years and by their very nature, tedious and long-winded: hence the backlog. However, I had occasion many times to be glad of the details that I had recorded like this and knew it was probably worth making the effort. The fruits of that long evening spent alone have now disappeared into the mists of time.

In spite of the children's usual nocturnal activities, I wasn't that tired and had got up early, feeling the pull of the wonderful morning outside. The sun was flooding through the house and I was eager to get out into the magic of the May morning. I sent Sophia and Christian off to sort out breakfast and headed for the shower.

As I was leaving for a business trip abroad the following day, I was determined to get the most out of the time we had together. When at home at the weekends in my garden in Kent, I often looked up at the planes crossing in the sky above and would think of the coming week and the next trip I would be taking for the bank. I tended to think of my life in the office merely as a role I was called upon to play and, in truth, I never really relished all the travelling my job involved. In fact, travel was much more Catherine's thing, whereas I preferred the tranquillity of the fields and the woods near home. With the windows wide open that morning and the sound of birds floating on the air, I couldn't wait to get outside.

I turned on the water. Halfway through, I suddenly heard a buzzing in my ears and realised I was starting to feel very strange. Just like that. No prior warning, no other symptoms. Absolutely fine, and then suddenly it felt as if the life blood was seeping out of me, which on reflection it probably was. I sank down and tried to steady myself but whatever was going on didn't feel as if it was going to go away. In fact, I rapidly began to feel worse and worse. With trembling hands, I pulled down a towel and, willing my wobbly feet forward, I stumbled back to bed. I was beginning to worry. This didn't feel like anything I had ever experienced before. My thoughts rushed ahead to the following day, the day after the bank holiday, when I was supposed to leave for Germany on a business trip. I began to wonder what my colleagues at work would think when I didn't turn up. Already I had a suspicion that something pretty serious was happening.

Lying there, wrapped in a towel and unable to conquer the creeping weakness that was invading my body, I began to feel the possible seriousness of my predicament. Catherine was due to return later that day, but for the moment, I was in the house alone with Sophia and Christian and would need to think about what to do with them if this sensation didn't pass. As I lay there trying to recover myself, I had to admit that I was feeling very strange and unwell and decided there and then that I would have to do something to make sure that they would be OK, as I was feeling more and more unable to function properly. Christian's classmate and his brother were due to come that morning to play with him. I told him to call the boys' parents and ask them to change the arrangements, as I obviously didn't feel in a fit state to be able to manage such a lively gang. Fortunately, the boys' parents suggested that it would be better to come and collect Christian and keep him with them until I felt better, and that they would soon be on their way.

Sophia very sweetly brought me breakfast in bed, but I couldn't eat anything. The two of them sat on the bed next to me and did their best to make me feel better. They had never seen me ill in their whole lives and I knew that this was a shock for them.

I felt dreadfully nauseous and the noise in my ears hadn't stopped. Suddenly I was very sick. I knew I couldn't stand up or try to make it to the bathroom. Sophia gave me the bin beside the bed, and when I had finished she calmly cleaned me up. I remember thinking that she should have been spending the day laughing and hanging out with her friends like a normal thirteen-year-old, instead of having to take the responsibility of her disintegrating father on her young shoulders. But she did, and she was amazing. In their turn, Lucia, sixteen, and Christian, only eight, would also rise to the occasion and show a love and maturity well beyond their years. It is not what a man dreams of for his children. But their response that day and each day since has certainly made me hugely proud and full of love for them.

Shocked to feel my strength ebbing away so rapidly, I tried to write down the time on a piece of paper, but, while doing so, I noticed that my handwriting was looking worse than ever. Sensing that I might have to see a doctor, and in a last-ditch attempt to keep up appearances, I managed to put on my jeans and removed all my credit cards but one from my wallet. Since I was due to leave for Germany the following day, I had already prepared my documents for the journey and had left them beside the bed. Reaching for them now, I grabbed my passport and German ID card. I found my donor card and put it in the wallet.

Quite alarmingly, I suddenly began to notice that I couldn't move my left side and, when I tried to speak, I knew I was sounding strange. I reached for the phone and called Catherine. My mother-in-law answered, and she must have been concerned, because I could hear the anxiety in her voice as she asked if I was all right. I said I wasn't and when Catherine came on the line I tried to tell her what had happened, but I was aware that my speech was really slurred. I knew I sounded drunk. As my words blurred into a mumble, Sophia took the phone and I tried to explain to her that I thought I had had a stroke. She repeated the words to Catherine in a slow and hesitating voice filled with incredulity and shock. Although I had not articulated the thought until this moment, I realised at that point that I was sure that this was indeed what was happening. Catherine immediately asked if I had called the doctor and, when I told her that I hadn't, she said that she would immediately do so. Sophia replaced the phone for me and the strange unrecognisable sound of my own voice reverberated on in my brain.

That would be the last time we spoke to each other. That hurried moment of panic and disbelief when I felt us stretching out to each other across the distance. From that moment on, speech and all capacity to make the slightest voluntary sound faded from me, the deafening silence enveloping me like an extra large coat, muffling out all sound and exiling me from any true expression of my self.

Beyond words, beyond touch, beyond life. The before now irrevocably divorced from the after.

After putting the phone down, I must have fainted. I don't know how long I was out of it, but I temporarily lost consciousness. When I came to, an ambulance team was there and Lucia had returned home with her friend's mother, Lena, who mercifully now stayed and took control of the situation. She promised to follow the ambulance to the hospital with Lucia and Sophia and to make sure that Christian was safely collected and looked after for the day. She assured me she would stay with them and take care of them till Catherine arrived and this was obviously a huge relief to me. The ambulance men then carried me downstairs to the waiting ambulance.

On arrival at the local accident and emergency department, I tried to explain to various doctors what had happened. One of them even asked me in German to try and tell him my version of events, but I couldn't manage to put two words together. The girls were kept away from me most of the time, and I later discovered that they were waiting in a side room and were not allowed to come close to me. Each time they tried to get near me they were sent away. As this phase went on for most of the day, they were very distressed at this, especially as no one explained to them or to Lena much of what was going on. In fact, I hardly saw anything of them all through that day until Catherine arrived. In spite of this, they had the courage to keep returning and to try to talk to me, only to be sent away each time. I had the distinct impression, as the day wore on, that no one was really sure what to do anyway and this added to my anxiety.

It was during the process of the first brain scan that I noticed my body becoming stiffer by the minute. After the scan I returned to A&E, and as by then I couldn't speak at all, I was pleased that the staff had given me a catheter. I knew from my father, who had had a stroke, that the bladder was going to be a problem. To compound the horror, I realised that now I couldn't move a single muscle any more. I seemed to have become entirely paralysed. My brain was spiralling into shock and panic. I couldn't grasp the objective reality of what was happening. Catherine was still hundreds of miles away and I desperately wanted her to be there with me. Moreover, since it was bank holiday Monday, the A&E department had a skeleton staff on duty, mainly junior doctors, and I was left alone for long periods of time. My thoughts raced and I fought hard to keep the terror down.

Then, with sudden clarity, I began to realise that the journey I had made to the hospital, via the old familiar country lanes, was a journey towards this moment. I saw the man I had left behind waking full of life to that wonderful May morning and asked myself how I would ever be able to find my way back to him.

In truth, it is someone I have longed to be, but whom I have never been able to find again.

My Long Day's Journey into Night

Pushing through the crowds, I stop the first uniformed guard I find and try to explain why I have to board the very next train to London. He looks into the blank pallor of my face. I see him trying to read the turmoil and confusion behind the expression. I struggle to tell him that my husband has suffered some kind of stroke and that I must get to the hospital as quickly as possible. With very few words, he takes my arm and steers me to a first-class compartment. He tells me to take a seat and to let him manage any irregularities about my standard ticket which is for a completely different train. There's a fog at the front of my brain and fear is making my heart beat very fast. I can't seem to understand all the words he is saying, but the look on his face scares me because he can see the seriousness of the situation that somehow my own brain is still denying.

Hasso's phone call just hours before opened a shaft below my feet and sent me plummeting into freefall. I sit and stare beyond the window as the train speeds forward, seeing nothing. My stomach feels nauseous, my head a jangle of terrifying voices clamouring for my attention. I hear, but strain to ignore what they are screaming at me.

Quite how I have come to be on the train at all is a result of frantic decisions after Hasso's call. I remember it had something to do with an abortive car journey into clogged bank holiday traffic and a dash for the nearest train station, but beyond the worried face of my mother as the train draws away from the platform and a dull pain somewhere at the centre of my chest, I am conscious of very little.

There is only an uncontrollable longing to annihilate the physical miles that lie between us. I want the countryside and the towns to fold themselves up, and time to slip and contract. The reality is unforgivingly slow and leaden. In the silence of the compartment where I sit alone for most of the journey, rigidly staring at the fields and villages ripping past the window, stiff and numb, no one can hear the demented clamour of the voices inside my head. I sit mute and bewildered as the voices fill the void, my own among them. At the front of the cacophony is my own insistent pleading. A kind of one-sided circular bargaining with a God whose existence I thought I had long since ceased to believe in. Let him come out of this. Let him be OK. Let him live. Maybe you want to take some of him, but, please, please, please, please, not all of him. Give him back to me. I'll do anything. Just don't let this be happening.

Outside the countryside extends ever onwards, but inside my head, time has concertinaed. While I am willing it to race and catapult me forward towards him across the miles, slicing the distance between us, it has transformed itself into treacle, a kind of sticky mud dripping in heavy clods. I imagine it turning itself inside out and returning us to yesterday, before the nightmare began, before I started this lunatic fall. Instead I seem to be creeping forward in slow motion. And all the time the voices, the pressure growing in my head, the falling sensation and an insidious worming in the pit of my stomach.

When I leave the train more than six unbearable hours and two changes later, I know instantly that all the inner pleading with a merciful God has been in vain. Our friend Lena is standing on the platform to meet me and her face shatters all my feeble hopes.

She has been with the children all day at the hospital. As she embraces me and tries to respond honestly to my pleas for news, her thinly veiled desperation tells me more than any words could.

It seems that I have indeed arrived. But it is not the destination I had hoped against hope for. The clarity of it is overwhelming. I have come to the place and the time where people suffer. Here is the truth of it.

As I push through the doors of the hospital and make urgent enquiries about where to find Hasso, I am again aware of the strange sensation of falling. The ground has gone from under my feet and I am tumbling into a darkness and a madness from which only his strong hand can save me. My heart tightens and I try to find him in the long row of beds in the casualty ward.

And, despite the ominous silence that has already smothered my prayer for a miracle, from somewhere inside me a tiny, stubborn glimmer of hope wriggles free. If I can find him, I urge myself to believe, if only I can come in time, perhaps he will not die. Perhaps he can save me, I think in my bewildered logic, if only I can get to him before it's too late.

But somewhere inside, on the edges of my brain, like a screw turning on my heart, lies the fear that maybe it is already too late.

I find him, finally, in a corner on the A&E department and am overwhelmed by this first sight of him. He tries to speak when he sees me but can only emit a long and heart-stopping sound that becomes a wail and ends in a sob. I am too shocked to allow my brain to accept what I am seeing and hearing as reality. He is struggling to breathe and I can't see any movement at all in his body. But it is his eyes that hold me. I see the desperate pleading in them. They follow me wherever

I move and are insistent in their effort to hold my attention. I struggle to get him to respond in some way to my questions. He can only reply with a terrible sobbing howl and the sound of this desperation turns my blood cold. I am in shock, but feel compelled to help him somehow to break through the barrier of silence. Since his eyes are the only thing he still appears to have any control over, it seems logical to get him to use them.

I tell him to open them if he can hear and understand. Immediately they open wide. I tell him to close them, and he does. I think for a moment. The panic is bubbling up through my chest.

'OK, don't worry about trying to talk, just open your eyes for yes and close them for no,' I suggest.

They open wide. It feels like a massive nod though his head has not moved one iota. I feel my heart stop for an instant. It is glaringly obvious that, though all his motor functions are out of action, his brain is working with perfect clarity. I catch my breath with the sudden realisation of both the joy and the horror of what this means.

'Good,' I try to smile encouragingly. 'I'm going to ask you some questions and you can tell me how you feel.'

Eyes wide open.

'Are you in pain?' The most important question of all.

Eyes open.

'A lot?'

Eyes closed.

'Thank God. Where does it hurt?' Stupid question, I realise, but it is out of my mouth before I can catch it back again. Of course, only yes/no questions are possible. I try again. 'In your chest?'

No.

'Your legs, your back, your arms . . .?' *No* to each of these.

'Your head?'

Yes.

'Oh God, that's awful! Can you bear it? Is it really bad? Do you want something for it?' Again, another stupid string of questions he can't answer. I am already feeling cross with myself. I straighten up and try to focus myself, bending my brain to adapt my questions to what he can answer.

No, he thinks he doesn't need any painkillers for now, but he isn't sure he can continue to bear it if it gets any worse.

We continue in this way for several hours, while the staff try to decide what to do. I search desperately for suitable questions and I'm increasingly aware of how crucial it is for me to get this right. So much depends on it.

Finally, Hasso's breathing difficulties become so bad that I experience a wave of terror as I see him struggling for breath. I run to find a doctor. My heart is pounding and I'm so scared that I can hardly get the words out. Suddenly, though, things begin to move fast. After a brief consultation, the doctors decide on sedation and the life-support machine.

Numbly, I watch as tubes are attached and machinery is hitched up to Hasso's body. Doctors and nurses busy themselves around his bed as I try to catch a glimpse of his face over their shoulders. His eyes are fixed steadily on mine, holding me and rooting me to the spot.

I have never felt so frightened and alone in all my life.

A & E

There were no words to describe the moment when Catherine finally arrived. By then, I was lying in a section of A&E separated by curtains from a few other critical patients, unable to move, to greet her, to explain what had happened or to speak any words to her at all. In addition, my breathing was getting more and more difficult and I was unable any more to keep the lid on my emotions. I was flooded with panic. All I could do was lie there as she hugged and kissed me. I could feel the wet tears on both our faces but could do nothing to wipe either hers or mine away.

It was clear that I wasn't going to make it at all, unless something was done. I had no way of knowing then what damage had already occurred in my brain and how life had now already changed irrevocably.

By about nine in the evening, more than twelve hours since the stroke had begun, the doctors finally reached the decision that it would be better to transfer me to another hospital where there would be specialists who could deal better with the situation. Catherine urged them to pull out all the stops. They got on the phone and rang around for several hours, but seemed to be taking ages to secure a bed.

In addition there was much hurried consultation over the phone between the junior doctors manning A&E and their superiors, who, it seemed to me, somehow never thought my condition serious enough to merit a visit or an examination from any of them. The junior doctors were left entirely in control. While we were waiting, a lumbar puncture was performed to determine what kind of stroke they were dealing with. But by now, my breathing had entered a critical stage and I was gagging for air. While all systems seemed to be shutting down, my brain was still functioning with absolute clarity. Terror flooded my whole being. Unable to move a muscle or utter a sound, I was now beginning to suffocate. The doctors decided to sedate me and put me on a respirator. As I lost consciousness, I recall that I experienced a huge sense of relief just to be able to drift away.

At around midnight, I was transferred by ambulance to central London. Catherine was not allowed to travel with me in the ambulance. Fortunately, some close friends had come to the hospital to offer their support and they kindly took her in their car behind the ambulance. The children were being safely looked after for the night, but as we later discovered they too were in a desperate state of trauma and worry.

Some Hours after Midnight,
1 May 2000, Central London

The hospital is dimly lit; a hush hangs over the endless corridors and swinging doors.

When I finally find where they have brought him, I enter a room where night and day are an irrelevance. Artificial low light maintains a clinical 24-hour world. Six beds: patients swathed in tubes, oxygen masks, wires. Machines whirring, clicking, beeping. Respirators rhythmically engender the rise and fall of invisible lungs, the mechanical life breath of real people suspended on the very edge. No one seems to be awake, but I am not sure if their sleep is the natural balm of exhaustion or a drug-induced coma.

They lead me to his bed. A landscape of white. His eyes are closed and his face is obscured by the breathing apparatus; he is a tangle of wires. He has been deeply sedated. Somewhere against the whiteness of the pillow, his hair, short though it is, appears tousled and distressed. The contours of his face flood me with a stab of recognition and realisation that jerks me from the torpor of shock. This is Hasso. And yet not Hasso. This cannot be him. I love him too much for this to be him.

The pump heaves breath in and out of his chest causing the sheet to rise and fall.

Where is he? I lower myself into the chair beside him. His hands lie on the crisp folded sheet, their bones and skin as familiar as my own. Slowly I reach out and lift one into mine. It is warm, smooth, yet heavy in its lifelessness. Habit waits for him to squeeze mine, envelop it into his and fold the fingers round his own, as he has always done. With my other hand I stroke his face and brow, trying to avoid the tubes. I touch his hair and lean in close to whisper into his ear. My hands, and, I realise, my whole body, are trembling.

His name. I say his name over and over. It is as if naming him will work some transformation, as if the word will travel to the inner recesses of that deep place where he now is and awaken him before he slips away. As if this one word will claim him as my own and bring him back to me. There is, after all, no way to sever us. We are bound to each other beyond all separation.

My lips can feel the light stubble on his cheeks that has grown throughout the day. The skin below is cool and clammy and his colour is faintly grey. But the roughness of his cheek quickens my heart. He may be in suspended animation, on automatic pilot, but his body isn't throwing in the towel. Nature keeps going. It is like a sign. Deep down his life has not given up on him. My stubbornly insistent brain tells me that the warmth of his hand and the beard on his face are tokens of resistance. I tell myself that a battle to hold on is raging within him, the apparent stillness of his exterior only belies the struggle.

I am gradually aware of a tight discomfort in my chest. I draw back a few inches and his face shifts into a different focus. I suddenly realise that my breathing has unconsciously slowed to the rhythm of the machine, keeping pace with the inward and outward flow from his lungs. My whole body is taut and tense. All day my subconscious mind has been tightening the vice in anticipation and dread of this moment.

His nurse is sweet and very kind. She returns to the bed every ten or fifteen minutes to adjust or check the machines or to attend to the tubes which appear to be attached to several areas of his body. The ward is a constant sea of muffled noise and restrained movement, yet strangely silent of real life.

Leaning forward in the chair, I let my head fall against the pillow and look at him as I have done every night for all the years we have known each other. His profile, chiselled and strong, gives me a moment of calm.

'Hold on, my love,' I whisper. 'Hold on.'

For what feels like an eternity I wait beside his bed, staring at his face, unable to leave for a moment in case he should wake up. Night turns into day. Doctors and nurses come and go. Minutes turn into hours. The waiting is unbearable.

When he finally opens his eyes it is a massive shock. Somehow, naïvely I suppose, I have been hoping that regaining consciousness would mean recovery, that his mobility and speech would be showing signs of slowly getting back to normal. I have been concentrating all my mental energies on willing him to return to me. I haven't allowed myself to contemplate the alternative.

When the hours of drug-induced sleep end and he is finally fully awake, I am confronted by the startling immobility of both his face and his body. Once so alive with expression and energy, he now lies there, stone-like and terrifyingly silent. My initial thought is that the drugs have probably induced some kind of deep immobility and I remember the short-lived paralysis I experienced after my Caesarean section. But there is a worrying similarity in his unresponsiveness to the state I found him in when I first arrived at the A&E department on the day of the stroke, which was, of course, hours before the doctors began sedating him. The same inability to move any part of his body, the same mute response to all my questions, the same terror in his eyes.

I try not to let him see that I am suddenly aware of my

stomach churning and my heart beating so loudly that it feels as if it is crushing my chest. The sight of his pallor and his probing, pleading eyes send me into light-headed panic. It seems that the intervening time while I have watched him sleep away the hours hasn't changed a thing. He is still paralysed and unable to speak. I hardly need to wait more than a few seconds to know that this is the real thing. I know that if he were able to, he would have spoken immediately. Taking my heart in my hands I ask him if he can see me.

Yes, his eyes blink. To my many other questions he responds that he is not in too much pain but that he can't move anything. His face looks calm. It is an illusion. His eyes communicate the terror. Yet in their searching intensity I also see an iron determination. He needs to find some way of communicating his thoughts and not simply of responding to my questions. Because it comes to me with shocking certainty at that moment that, no matter how hard I try, I will never be able correctly to predict his thoughts each time or to offer him the correct yes/no option. I suddenly feel utterly inadequate. Clearly, he will have to use me as his mouthpiece, as the conduit for his thoughts, but I am going to have to find a far better way than this. The questions are too haphazard and don't allow him to say what he wants.

I look at him in silence, desperately racking my brain for another way. There has to be a better idea. He could perhaps spell things to me? We could use the yes/no thing to spell out letters and I could transcribe his words. I feel the excitement quicken inside me. Until he can speak properly this clearly feels like the best option. I put it to him and he opens his eyes wide.

'A, B, C, D, E . . .?' I begin at once, enunciating the letters slowly and clearly sotto voce so as not to disturb the other patients. Then I realise I will have to write this down.

I rummage in my bag for a pen and a scrap of paper. I am eager for the first letters. This will be his first independent utterance without my clumsy prompting. I watch his eyes intently as I labour through the entire alphabet right through to Z without him blinking once. Clearly, something has gone wrong.

'Did I miss it?'

Yes.

'Shall I start again?'

Yes.

All the way through the alphabet again until I notice his eyes flutter. My heart falters. Is he telling me to stop? I'm not sure. I stop abruptly at Q. Q? But no sentence starts with a Q, I think. Well, not many, anyway. I stare at him with a puzzled expression on my face, trying to remain calm. Perhaps it wasn't Q. In fact, he opened and closed his eyes so imperceptibly that I'm not sure now if he had wanted P or Q or even O or R. Perhaps it wasn't any of them at all, perhaps his eyelids moved a fraction quite involuntarily. It is beginning to feel very difficult indeed.

'Is it Q?' I ask.

Eyes tightly shut. Damn, wrong again.

'Shall I go back and start again?' I venture tentatively, worried that the frustration might result in him losing heart from the outset.

No.

'Shall I go from L again?'

Yes.

And so we begin again from L. He is tiring fast with each letter, especially when I make a mistake and have to go back once, twice, even three times. His efforts leave him exhausted and the muddle is frustrating us both. My page is crowded with letters and crossings out and I am feeling dizzy and desperate in the stuffy air of the ward.

'I'm so sorry,' I whisper, leaning forward to let his un-responsive lips touch my face. I want to cry, to scream, to wail. More than anything I want him to lift his hand and stroke my head. Nothing happens. I can feel his shallow breath against the side of my cheek. He wants to say something. He is trying so hard. I have to pull myself together and carry on.

I sit back and try to decipher what I have. There is a P, an O (possibly), an A, a K, an M (I'm not at all sure about that one), an E and an A. The truth is I don't know if it is one word or two, whether it is some kind of code, a name, an abbreviation, a question or even a request. He is staring at me, willing me to understand.

'OK,' I suggest, 'I'll read each letter to you and you tell me if it's right or wrong.'

Eyes wide open.

'Right, I've got a P . . .?'

No.

'Not P?'

No.

I remember I wasn't sure about the P. I look at the next letter.

'Does it start with O?'

Yes.

Phew, at least we have the first letter. We have been at it half an hour already.

'Is the next letter an A?'

Yes.

'Then K?'

Yes. He is looking at me so intently now, willing me with every fibre to see it. Suddenly, all on their own, as if by magic, the letters rearrange themselves on the page and the word leaps out at me. I look up at him and, in spite of all my efforts, the tears begin running down my face.

'It's Oaklea!' I whisper. 'Oaklea.'

The name of our house. His eyes open so wide at this and the tears that well up in them fill me with such sadness that I can't speak. Just one word, but it means so much.

Intensive Treatment Unit

When I finally regained consciousness the following day, I was in intensive care, in London. Clearly, I was 'alive again', but it didn't really feel like it to me. I was hitched up to tubes and machines, over my face was a mask connected to a respirator and, when I tried to move and speak, I could find nothing in my body that would respond.

Catherine was there beside my bed and she tried to explain what had happened. The blankness of my response must have been earth-shattering in the extreme. I have subsequently joked with her that, at that point, she thought I had completely lost my marbles, as she was earnestly asking me questions and getting me to use my eyes to respond to her. My mind, however, was well and truly intact. Curiously, although paralysed everywhere, I could still open and close my eyes and, minimal though it was, this was the only movement I could control. It was startlingly clear to Catherine, right from the beginning, that, in spite of how unresponsive I may have looked in terms of facial expression and lack of speech, my mental state was totally unaffected. Indeed, I was able to understand everything that was going on.

It is true to say that I could feel and remember everything that had happened totally clearly. I started 'reviewing the situation', my inner voice running over the events of the previous day in both German and English, a dual monologue which has continued in me ever since. What, then, actually was the damage to the little grey cells? The way I saw it, it was all horribly clear. I couldn't even sit without support. I was totally without movement and was unable to make a sound. That was pretty bad, but inevitably worse was to come.

Every morning, the doctors and nurses in ITU would gather for a meeting to discuss the patients. Additionally, a consultant, accompanied by several doctors, would visit once a week. Finally, after several days in this surreal state, the 'Gods in White' visited me and pronounced my fate. They told me that I had had a stroke in the brainstem. They explained that this had also resulted in something known as 'locked-in syndrome'.

What on earth did this mean? My thoughts immediately went back to the biology lessons I had had at school. When discussing the role of the brainstem, the teacher had mentioned that severe damage in this area would normally result in death, as it is the narrow pathway through which all messages and functions from the brain pass to the rest of the body. An event as serious as a stroke resulting from a blockage was therefore seriously bad news and it was clear to me that I shouldn't have survived it. But what this total entrapment of the mind in a weak, unresponsive body actually meant to me was quite another issue and I would spend the next few days and weeks discovering that. It was, however, abundantly clear that my muscles, which had taken a lifetime to build up through steady exercise and movement, were already rapidly wasting away.

For now, though, thoughts about long-term disability were simply too monstrous to grasp and refused to take on any sense of reality. I was overwhelmed by a numbing kind of disbelief. Unbeknown to me, of course, the harsh reality of life as 'The Man in the Iron Mask' was waiting in the wings;

but, at this stage, it was something I was almost unable to comprehend. For the moment it was far too appalling to contemplate.

The days passed and I lay in suspended animation. I realised that I was still in ITU and had not been moved on with most of the other patients. I was consumed with anxiety. When the doctors visited again, I was told that they did not understand my lack of progress and that, compared with other similar patients, it looked as if I had something like a one in five chance of recovery. These words, clinical and harsh, seemed to be accompanied somewhere in the distance by the deafening sound of the door to my real self and my real life slamming shut. They were to become engraved on my heart and would come to haunt me ever after.

Communicating

Having realised that Hasso can recruit his eye blinks to communicate, we struggle on for days in the same fashion. Eyes open for 'yes', eyes closed for 'no'. I sit beside the bed intoning the alphabet, letter after letter, and try to catch the flickering movements of his eyes. Hasso is immensely patient with my bumbling blunders, but is often unable to remain conscious for long enough to complete a word or short sentence. His many attempts frequently end in a depressing dead end and, although I sometimes manage to get the gist of several words, more often than not the sentence has to be abandoned. The whole process is immeasurably taxing for him. There has to be a better way than this very hit-and-miss, long-winded affair. But it is true that we have made the breakthrough. And it is an extremely important one. A tiny, tiny chink has been forced in the wall of the silence engulfing him and it is his voice and his thoughts that are coming through it. It feels like the most enormous triumph over fate. And the need to continue becomes an imperative.

But there is no disguising how difficult the whole process is. And there is another problem. So far, only I seem able to communicate with him like this. The time and attention it requires are beyond everyone else so, inevitably, I become the only means he has of communicating with everyone else around him.

Almost ten days, now, since the stroke. It's late. I'm trying to complete a sentence with him before finally leaving him for the night. The ward is empty of visitors and many patients are already asleep. The staff have long since got used to my ignoring the set visiting hours and are amazingly tolerant of my presence. One of the male nurses quietly approaches me with a sheet of laminated paper and gives it to me, explaining that they found it on another ward in the file of a patient who left the hospital some time ago. He thinks it might help.

I look at the sheet. It is a simple grid of letters arranged into rows and columns. I study it for a few moments and then it dawns on me. Each column is headed by a vowel which has underneath it the subsequent consonants. Five columns of unequal length. Instead of going through the whole alphabet each time, if we use this system we could speed things up immensely. I could offer Hasso the choice of the five vowels A, E, I, O, U and, according to the vowel chosen, then the letters below it. So, if he selected E, for example, the next choice would only be between E, F, G or H. There would be no need to go through the whole alphabet with each word.

A	E	I	O	U
B	F	J	P	V
C	G	K	Q	W
D	H	L	R	X
		M	S	Y
		N	T	Z

The best ideas are often the simplest ones and the sheer clarity of this one has won me over immediately. It is simple, but brilliant. Moreover, anyone can learn how to use it and this will open up Hasso's communication immeasurably. It won't take long to master the rows and columns and anything that will make the process easier and less of a strain for Hasso is priceless.

We waste no time in getting started. The difference it makes is immense. The words appear on my page, haltingly at first, until Hasso has mastered the chart in his head, but within a day or two, so rapidly that whole sentences are taking the same time as we have spent up to now on single words. There is still the problem of confused letters and of not knowing where one word ends and another begins. But this method is immensely superior to the other. It is like unleashing the floodgates. Sentence after sentence pours out of him covering everything from important messages about his pain and discomfort to advice on the household finances. He asks questions about the children and the family, gives me pin numbers for bank accounts and relays instructions for his office and staff at work. He tells me moving and intensely painful things about his emotions and even tries a few bits of humour. I realise that now, suddenly, he will be able to communicate a little through me with his visitors when they are allowed to see him and to dictate short messages to the children and letters to his parents.

Imperfect as it is, this method of communication is for the moment literally all that we've got. In spite of all our hopes and prayers, his voice, the voice I love so much, seems to have vanished. But he has at least proved himself stronger than the tyranny of the silence that has surrounded him till now.

Life on Intensive Care

My experience of life on the intensive treatment unit was of one disturbing event after another. The decision was made to perform an operation under anaesthetic, in order to fit a feeding tube into my stomach (a gastrostomy) to enable them to keep me alive with liquid feeds. The required procedure was to be conducted in a nearby hospital, but an anaesthetist would accompany me. This doctor very much reminded me of the deputy in our finance department who, coincidentally, had left the bank to go into medicine. Though awake, I was by now so full of drugs and sedatives that their effect was beginning to influence my perception of things. In my strange state, I pondered if this was her or someone else entirely. This was not the only time that I would be reminded of people in the outside world beyond my reach. As the operation was scheduled for first thing in the morning, I had to start the day early. But in the nether world of ITU, I was already very disorientated. While I was being prepared for the operation, I was told that I was about to have a 'peg' fitted. Strange word, I thought. I had no idea that a gastric feeding tube is actually also known as a PEG (percutaneous endoscopic gastrostomy). No one seemed to think it necessary to enlighten me further or to explain what it would mean to me in the future and, since I couldn't ask, the operation went ahead without my really knowing what on earth was going on. As far as I was aware, it felt as if something resembling a sort of service check had been done during the operation and a kind of chain had been attached to my stomach. My lucky charm? As it was, it could have been anyone's guess what they were doing because, as I couldn't move my head, I couldn't see what was going on around me anyway.

Once the operation was over, I was returned to ITU. As the days passed, Catherine, and often the children, sat with worried expressions at my bedside, held in suspended animation and frozen in a state of fear and disbelief. Hours merged into days. Days merged into nights. They kept vigil. Life had come to a complete stop.

We were looked after on a one-to-one basis during the day. It seemed to me that the job description for working here began with a requirement for nurses to be from the southern hemisphere, as the majority of the staff, apart from my Finnish nurse and another English male nurse, appeared to be Australians. All the nurses worked to a strict rota every day, which at least kept the element of surprise going, while making as many nurses as possible aware of our needs.

Life went on in its inexorable fashion and I began to see a sort of routine in it. The hospital bed I was in was too short, but I was used to that. It's a common problem I face in England. I am only 1.89 m tall which is barely average among some of the British youth of today, but the beds were all standard length and made no concessions for tall people. So the lower half of my legs and my feet were always left hanging over the end of the bed. Really uncomfortable when you can't move at all.

Every morning, most of the patients were visited by therapists and/or doctors. We were all measured up and all of us ended up with some kind of appliance or other. Leg splints seemed to be the most common among them. The bays in our area were not all the same size and one of the numerous visitors of a lady in the middle complained that I had a bigger bay. To make matters worse, there was also a guy called Hassan next to me and everyone kept mixing us up. At least my new life had its little diversions.

The stroke had affected much more than my ability to move, as I was to discover bit by bit. Everybody on ITU had a TV set going all the time, except of course for me. No one had seen fit to offer me a TV, as it was assumed that I wouldn't be able to see it properly. I found it incredibly irritating to be surrounded by wall-to-wall television, day and night, which I couldn't see. I didn't realise at this stage that, even if I had had one, I still would not have been able to see the wretched screen anyway.

I was soon forced to face the music again. One morning a team of speech therapists arrived at my bedside in a flurry of great excitement. In an effort to facilitate communication for me we were presented with the latest in modern technology – a spelling machine which was activated by eye blinks through huge glasses, which in turn were linked to the machine. This was hugely promising, but my enthusiasm rapidly turned to disappointment. My problem was really quite basic, as I couldn't even see the cursor on the small screen. I could see some of the letters, and was sometimes able to activate the machine, but only at random. Clearly, despite all the great hopes for this assistive technology, this device wasn't going to get me very far. Reluctantly, I had to admit defeat and accept that, if my range of movement was indeed so very limited, then even technology wouldn't be able to improve things much.

About this time, I developed recurring bouts of hiccups, which became a terrible scourge and, in desperation, one nurse even tried to combat them with a hairdryer! The hiccups kept recurring every ten minutes or so, and even seemed to follow a detectable pattern. Much later on, when I was allowed an abortive attempt to swallow a few spoonfuls of yoghurt, the hiccups usually made the food fall out of my mouth and go all over my face. This generally caused quite a stir, not to mention a considerable mess of the therapist's clothing. To general relief, however, this finally wore off after some months.

However, the penny still didn't drop completely. Hope kept driving me on from day to day, and my instinct for survival would not allow me to let go of the belief that things would, must . . . no, absolutely had to, improve sooner or later.

For the first few weeks, hearing was also a major problem. On one side, I couldn't hear at all. It was also very difficult to get this message across as, due to the position of my bed, Catherine and any other visitors tended to stand on my deaf side to talk to me. Spelling out that I couldn't actually hear on that side was far from easy, as I couldn't hear the letters properly when Catherine went through them, and was hence unable to respond with the correct eye blinks to spell out the message. It was many days before she realised what I was trying to say.

At this point in time, I was still connected up to the respirator with all manner of tubes, and it was decided that tests would have to be performed to ascertain whether or not I could breathe independently. Needless to say, I didn't make the grade. This was another bleak and cruel moment of realisation. I was informed that a tracheotomy would have to be carried out. A tracheotomy is an incision into the trachea (windpipe) that forms a temporary or permanent opening. The opening itself is referred to as a tracheostomy and this is usually shortened in hospital jargon to 'trachi'. To put it bluntly in layman's terms, then, my throat was cut. During the operation a device is inserted into the windpipe, sticking upwards and out of your throat, through which you are then supposed to breathe, and this is covered with a kind of removable filter known, curiously, in that hospital at least, as a 'Swedish nose'. This was to act as my new means of breathing for the better part of a year, but to me it also sealed off any hopes of returning to normality. I had erroneously hoped that it might help me to make some kind of sound, but of course this was not the case. I now had to confront the fact that from now on, I would be condemned to the role of 'The Quiet Man' forthwith.

The stroke had rendered me utterly mute.

I had a lot of dreams while in ITU and many of them were so strange I was often unable to disentangle one from another, but I want to mention a few. I had one recurring dream that seemed to lift me far beyond the confines of the ward and transport me to the rainy streets of New York. I remember trying to work out what I should do with the white poodle I found myself holding. It was wearing a red collar covered with black polka dots. I was distinctly aware that my surroundings belonged not to the modern world, but to the New York of the 1920s. People were standing round in a place that resembled Central Park, in large white, crowded tents, arranged in neat rows like a Roman bivouac. I never really worked out why these images kept recurring to me, but they would float up from time to time, no doubt as the staff topped up whatever it was they were sedating me with.

In another dream, this time a daydream which tormented me continuously, I was lying on a huge figure which lifted its stomach, and me, up and down with every breath. This time I knew perfectly well who the black figure with red skin was. I realise now that my subconscious was an impenetrable scene of struggle, where the Devil pursued me in the darkness in various guises. On other occasions he came as a raven. He insisted that all I had to do was to agree to go with him and everything would stop. I kept refusing, but the visions wouldn't go away.

The worst dream I had was actually quite a nightmare and

was about two similar incidents, one in Cornwall, the other in France. Several lorry drivers had had terrible accidents, and their brains were all that had survived the carnage. These were lying in buckets and were somehow linked up to their bodies, which were lying on small, rectangular trolleys. I can remember the great care that had to be taken not to mix them up. It was crucially important not to get the brains and the bodies confused. I remember that the French lorry driver's remains were somehow buried by something and I could see that he had died. His brain and his body had been separated. The brain disconnected from the body. For me the ultimate horror of death in life.

These kinds of dreams filled my waking and sleeping hours and were something I couldn't communicate, even to Catherine. They were so awful and so frequent. I was afraid that if I had tried to describe them, people would have thought that my mind had been seriously damaged. Even with the spelling system, I was unable to find the words to encompass them. They simply remained my constant companions every time I closed my eyes . . . and even when I didn't.

Within a day or so, my brother and my two sisters had flown in from Germany. In spite of the horror of all that had happened and the looks of fear and worry on their faces, it was so good to see them. I realised then that I had thought I would not come through and that I believed that, in all likelihood, I would never see them again. Their being there meant so much to me, even though they were only able to stay a few days before returning home. It was a very emotional time and before I knew it, Catherine was alone with me again and they were gone. I wondered quite seriously after that if I would ever see them again.

Catherine's main worry was that she had to leave the children behind in order to spend the time with me. This gnawed away at her every day. Not only was she with me all day long and many nights, she also had a good three hours of travel, up and down to London, seven days a week to cope with too. The children were obviously in a state of shock and needed her to be around. The dilemma was agonising. This was greatly alleviated by the incredible response of her parents. On the very evening of the first day, they had travelled up from Devon to take over looking after our children. They put no limit on the time they would stay. They simply wanted to make things as bearable as possible for the children, and to enable Catherine to get up to London each day. In practice, this meant that she spent the entire day next to my bed, leaving normally at around 11 p.m., or often simply staying the night next to me in an armchair. They also came to ITU to visit me as soon as possible, and assured me that they would stay on as long as was necessary. 'However long it takes,' they said. In fact, it was to be a whole year before they were able to return home, and not once did they complain, or make us aware of their own very real problems, which, since they were in their seventies and eighties, were to prove very serious in themselves.

During this eleven–day period in intensive care, I inhabited a strange and disturbing nether world, and was largely unaware of the extent to which the trauma–induced dreams and hallucinations I was experiencing kept leaking into my per-ception of reality. Much of what I remember (according to Catherine) actually happened, but my awareness of it in the first few days was quite strange.

It was only when I came towards the end of this eleven-day period that the sedative drugs were finally withdrawn, and I began to emerge from this nightmare perception of things and was able to distinguish hallucination from reality.

Understanding of the gravity of my condition was not something that came immediately, as my mind seemed to be locked in total shock and rebellion against realising how awful things actually were. It was not until the fourth day that the realisation of the dreadful immobility hit me properly. It was a very strange feeling, a regression to a state even further back than babyhood, where I now found myself unable to yell, wriggle, eat or drink.

One small example of how the immobility affected my whole body in such a strange way was my left heel, which rapidly became completely numb. It began to feel as if I had something like an overlay of plastic on my skin. Then there was my right index finger. The stiffness I still experience in it has caused many subsequent problems, and I am now unable to straighten it at all. It is bent and crooked and when manipulated will only move in tandem with the middle finger. The resulting unintentional gesture can be misinterpreted by those around me who don't realise what is going on and I have found the potential for misunderstanding quite comical at times.

As the days rolled on, I experienced growing waves of spasms accompanied by stiffness and numbness, together with frequent acute pains in my head which felt like enormous explosions. The doctors began to think this might in fact be indicative of another more sinister event, so in order to assess the evidence a further brain scan was carried out. This showed no clear evidence of a second stroke but they explained that it was quite possible that these scans did not yet show the full picture of events inside my head. Only time would tell how serious these sensations might prove. So I could only assume that the horror I had experienced during those bouts of head pain and body seizures were like aftershocks following the first major quake.

Whatever it was that was actually going on, it was finally becoming clear to me, however, that my very own 'first circle of hell' was beginning to close in around me.

To the Ends of the Earth

He stares at the ceiling. Eyes barely open. I sit beside him, my field of vision only remotely conscious of the busy ward on the edges of my consciousness, my own eyes fixed on his. In the background the ever-present hissing rhythm of the life-support machine.

I try to imagine myself into his thoughts. Try to strain and shift the focus of my brain to follow him beyond the pain swimming in the recesses of his eyes.

I wait. We wait.

The waiting and the silence hang in a heavy veil around us, thickening the air and slowing down time.

Bizarrely, the echoes of a recent conversation we had a few days before with a friend filter through my head. Hasso had been talking about the time we came to live in England fourteen years before. He had thrown back his head and laughed when the friend suggested that he had left Germany and come to live in England because I'd persuaded him to. Then his face relaxed a little, losing some of the smile, but not quite.

'A lot of people think that,' he said, 'but there are a lot of people who don't know me. Including some who are quite close to me. It wasn't like that.' He stole a glance across the room at me and winked.

True, I thought, very true. There were plenty of people

who thought they understood him, but he always kept some-thing back, something private, something that only belonged to us.

Looking at him now through his lowered lids, I see his eyes fixed on the ceiling above our heads and they are moving almost imperceptibly, like a sleeper in a near-waking dream. They flit and tremble in tiny rapid movements as if surveying the far-off horizon. I try to travel with them, but know I can't. I want to see what he sees, think what he thinks, share the burden of the anguish. Carry it for him. Just for a moment.

What I do see shot through the clefts of memory is the light as it catches the blue of his eyes and the broad shape of his shoulders as he leans in towards me, inclining his body forward in his chair. We are sitting on the terrace of our house in Germany in early summer. He has come home after a particularly trying day at the office. Pulling off his tie and throwing his suit jacket over the back of the sofa, he has fallen into the wicker chair and stretched his long legs out in front of him. He takes a deep breath of the warm summer air and looks at me through the low, dipping sunlight, squinting as he does so into the late afternoon rays.

Through the cold artificial light of the intensive care ward, beyond the stiff, unnervingly still form of his long body stretched out below the crisp white sheet, I see him now as he was on that day, all animation and excitement despite the immense tiredness of a young father whose nights are broken by his first child and whose working day is long and tedious. I see him looking at me through the fluid, warm sunlight and feel the anticipation in his taut body.

It's understandable, I suppose, that people might think I talked him into moving to England. What they don't know is that Hasso had been planning to leave Germany long before I came into his life.

When we first met, he was keen to move abroad for a while

and he had been putting out feelers through the bank for a transfer into international audit. There had been some discussion about Argentina, possibly London or even the USA, but nothing concrete. He knew that it would be good for both of us, but was reluctant to talk about it too much with me until things were more definite. With no solid transfer offers emerging one year into our marriage, and the prospect looming of yet another year in the same job, he thought long and hard about the alternatives. Unbeknown to me, he was considering other options and spending a lot of time thinking of ways to achieve a move. He was by then set on England. After living with me for over a year, his English had improved immensely and he was confident that he could turn his hand to any job. Of course, he knew that I'd like the idea, but he still didn't confide in me. He wanted to test his own resolve and be sure his skills were adequate before he took the plunge. It wasn't until then that he decided to tell me.

That day on the terrace I knew something was up from the excited smile on his face.

'How would you feel about moving to England?' he asked, letting the words drop carefully into the space between us.

I don't remember what I said, but I do remember looking at him for ages and ages not knowing what to reply. He just sat there staring at me, smiling that broad smile and squinting into the sun. I knew that it was pointless asking him if he was sure. I knew him well enough by then to realise that he would have made his mind up once and for all before even talking to me and that all he wanted was for me to agree. I do remember that after a while we both started laughing and that I got up and went over to him, both of us giggling with the sheer craziness of it. We were young enough to find the virtual impossibility of what he was suggesting the best thing about it. He didn't have a job in England, we had a new baby, we'd have to give up the house he had bought at such a young age and become so attached to and look for another one in England. Added to that, we didn't have a penny to our name.

It's that smile I see now beyond the whirring of the machines and the blank stillness of the hospital bed. I see the tiny laughter lines around his eyes as I remember leaning down towards the long bulk of him in that wicker chair and putting my arms around his neck and hugging him. I can feel the tense excitement in him and the warm sunshine on his back. 'England's fine,' I say, 'just fine . . . more than fine!' We laugh and hug again. Then, in my memory, I take a step back and look at him. I see his right foot slightly lifted off the ground and his right leg jiggling up and down as it always does when he's concentrating or excited. He is still smiling and I know suddenly that he's been planning this for ages.

Today, beside his hospital bed, I also know that nothing has changed. For the truth is I'd have followed him to Outer Mongolia or darkest Africa. The only preposterous thing to me would have been the idea of doing anything at all without him. As I looked into his smile that day I felt it again. That electric streak of knowledge that whatever he decided, wherever he went, I wanted to be there. He could have asked me to go with him to the remotest corner of the world and I wouldn't have hesitated. And he knew it too. I didn't care what happened as long as we were together and, with the reckless confidence of youth, that seemed more than enough to make us both happy.

After all, we were twenty-five years old and life was sweet. And we, of course, were immortal.

PART TWO

The First Circle of Hell

Mid-May to July 2000

Life on the Ward

My time in intensive care finally came to an end. Eleven days had passed in ITU and there had been no sign of the much-hoped-for improvements. Eventually, it was decided to make room for someone else, so I was moved on. Not to a high-dependency ward, which would have been the most suitable place for me, but, because the hospital didn't have one, I was simply transferred onto a general ward. It was here that I was to experience the very worst, along with (in terms of a few very special people) some of the best, of hospital life. There were a number of horrors in store for me of which I was totally unaware at this point. The first shocks, though, were not long in coming.

At first, it was the deceptive nature of the relative silence that struck me on the ward. This was, of course a total misconception. Intensive care is a world of 24-hour light, constantly bleeping life-support machines, nurses coming and going and windowless unreality. There appears to be no difference between night and day. Insomnia, I have since learned, is a very typical symptom of the brainstem stroke I had suffered, but I had somehow felt at the time that the ward would provide me with the peace and quiet I so needed in order to be able to sleep. Of course, I had been told to expect that things would be different here, and had been led to believe that this would all be for the better. I couldn't have been more wrong.

The ward was divided into four large bays, each occupied by six patients who were crammed into the minimum of space. Each person's bed was so close to the next one that it was difficult to draw the curtains around the bed to get a modicum of privacy without enveloping the next-door patient, chairs and visitors in swathes of curtain. I was placed in a bay directly opposite the ward sisters' desk, so that they could 'keep an eye' on me. It might as well have been in Timbuktu, however, because the nurses never seemed to take much notice of me anyway.

I was surprised that one of the nurses was German and actually came from near a place not far from where I was born. In time I was to learn that the desperate crisis in staffing in hospitals in the UK meant that nurses were being recruited from many European countries and from very far beyond. The worst results of this shortage would impact on me in a very personal way in the shape of the so-called 'agency nurses', whose presence Catherine and I would both come to dread. In the meantime, however, the appearance of a German nurse on the ward certainly made it easier for my family in Germany to make enquiries about me.

The patients on this ward, even the most severely incapacitated of them, could all move about a fair bit. Unlike them, due to my immobility, I was at serious risk of developing bed sores. Consequently, I was told that I was to have a new bed with an air mattress. One evening, after Catherine had left, it was delivered and put together on site, where it soon developed a life of its own. I was at first pleased and somewhat impressed to get such a high-tech bed, but I couldn't have imagined the devious plan it had in store for me. At first, it lay low, probably in order to lull me into a false sense of security. Then, suddenly, the head and foot sections sprang up together like a closed book. That would have been fine by me, but for the fact that I was actually lying on the bed at the time. Indeed, to make matters worse, the bed still had more in store for me, as it wasn't long before the mattress itself began to deflate and go as flat as a pancake, leaving me with head and legs right up in the air on a hard metal base. As I couldn't make a sound, I had to wait to be rescued.

The next nasty surprise was waiting just around the corner. On most days I was hoisted from my bed into a wheelchair. I discovered that I had totally lost all head control. This was extremely disconcerting. Moreover, because the staff could not come up with a satisfactory solution for supporting my head, it had to be held at all times, like that of a small baby. I joked with myself that this was the next best thing to being seen 'hanging dead over a fence', but it really was not that funny. Just when I thought things couldn't get much worse, I found how wrong I was.

I was slowly beginning to get acquainted with some of the other characters on the ward, who inevitably reminded me, if ever I forgot, that this was a neurological hospital where many of the patients were not that sane. Once in a while, a man drifted into my bay, touched me and started to cry, usually to be led away by an apologetic nurse. My family has told me that I should also mention the following two gentlemen who, thankfully, usually conducted their business out of my view. One of them used to move up and down the ward miming powerful breast strokes, convinced he was swimming, while the other one had a habit of continually taking his trousers off and hiding them anywhere he could, including down the toilet. Inevitably, the extreme nature of what I saw around me on a daily basis made me ask myself what on earth I had come to.

During my time in this hospital there was a Spanish male nurse who was particularly kind to me. He always tried to find the time to chat to me and to spell a couple of words out with me. He did not find this easy and we both often got totally tied up and confused, especially when I realised that he was using the spelling chart the wrong way round. We got there in the end, however, but it was often hit and miss and sometimes quite hilarious. In spite of that, though, I'll never forget him for his kindness and for the way he came to say goodbye to me when he left. There were tears in his eyes and his voice was shaking. He held my hand warmly and shook it while he looked into my eyes. He was so moved and I could tell that he felt it very deeply. It was a moment that has stayed with me.

To compensate for the complete loss of my world, I found myself resorting to the age-old habits of prisoners rebelling against confinement. I began to journey in my mind. My thoughts often returned to life on the outside and particularly to memories of my various business trips. The busy, stressful environment of international banking that had been my element now seemed a world away, but I still felt very much part of that world and was mentally still in step with what would be going on at the office. On frequent occasions my brain would be 'at work' in the office in London and I still occupied the many hours of my new inertia mentally planning business trips, or problem-solving my way through the mesh of issues between London and Frankfurt.

My thoughts also often took flight to the times I had spent in our Hong Kong branch and for some reason memories of that time haunted me a lot. I recalled that at this time of year it would be very humid and well into the snake season. The abundance of snakes did not actually require protective footwear to be packed, as one may have thought, because in Hong Kong snakes are regarded as a delicacy. Actually, everything remotely edible usually ends up being caught and cooked out there. My first encounter with Hong Kong made me realise how much I had to learn about the place. There were so many fascinating traditions and customs. Red horses, for example, are supposed to bring good luck – and fish, it is believed, 'eat away' bad luck. I was amazed to discover a skyscraper with a huge hole, the size of a football pitch, in the middle of the building – designed that way, I was told, to avoid obstructing the flight path of a feeding dragon! My Chinese informant assured me that the dragon would be able to fly straight through the gap, and that this was fine because it was quite in line with what the Feng Shui master had advised.

When I first went out there on business, I bought an English/Chinese phrase book in the misguided hope that it might help me make a good impression, at least by making an effort to communicate with the locals. However, from the blank looks on the faces of my victims, it soon became obvious that something was seriously wrong. They clearly did not understand a word I was saying. My phrase book contained perfect examples of the dialect of Chinese spoken in Beijing but, as soon became apparent, certainly not the kind spoken here. In my ignorance I had forgotten that Hong Kong was, of course, sufficiently distant from the capital to have developed its own kind of Chinese. At least that's the explanation I gave myself, to avoid complete deflation of my ego.

Quite contrary to my expectations, for someone who hates city life, I actually found myself rapidly falling under Hong Kong's spell. The most stunningly breathtaking urban views in the world are to be had there and I never tired of contemplating the sight of the city laid out before me, especially at night.

Starting with the layered descent from the Peak at sunset, as the light dissolves quickly through the hardly existing dusk into the lukewarm night, looking in the direction of Kowloon and the New Territories on the mainland, thousands of miles and now a world away, I often found my mind's eye indulging in the contemplation of well-remembered sights. The time and the place at which you begin your tour scarcely seem important, as the effect is always stunning. From the moment you step onto an observation platform to see your surroundings, it feels as if you are surveying the world from the crow's nest of a schooner. The bird's-eye view before you, however, makes you realise that in fact this could be nowhere else on earth.

First you see the private residences of the well-heeled and famous; then, as the eye descends, there are the buzzards looking for prey. Then the tops of the skyscrapers and, further down, the big red flag on a rectangular-shaped cube, supported by just one leg – the Prince of Wales Building. From there one can see the last private house, sitting like a crown on a hill, the home of the former Governor. After that, the roof of Government House which, even after the Handover, still houses the administration. Further below come the footbridges, mostly covered, immediately followed by the double-decker trams and, down a bit, the red taxis in droves. Moving on, the eye comes across the helipads situated on reclaimed land, the ample hotel pools, where, in the morning, you can see various individuals silently practising their Tai Chi in solitude. Finally, there are the numerous passenger ferries of the Circle Line criss-crossing the South China Sea.

This whole scene is only occasionally interrupted by a junk, ploughing its way through this 'Waterworld', on the way back from the island of the golden Buddha, a veritable collision of the ancient and the modern, as it passes the world's largest container terminal and the tourist luxury liners from the other side of the island, Aberdeen way. My attention was often caught by the chains of lights of one particular vessel, marking a line between bow and stern over the masts, enlarging the silhouette of this hugely impressive ship. The contrast here could hardly have been greater. This ship was moored next to the floating detention centre for Vietnamese 'boat people'. An emblem of capitalism next to one of utter deprivation.

Standing on the viewing platform watching all of this, I would gaze at the lights illuminating the lives of the returning passengers against the backdrop of massive neon signs and colourful, flashing advertisements. Lying in my hospital bed, I could still feel the swell of the sea with every breath I took. Strange how my brain worked. I suddenly recalled how the illuminations had reminded me of a story a Spanish friend of mine had told me about the reason why Vauxhall Nova cars could only be marketed in Spain under a different name. Like these lights flashing on and off, the name Nova made people think the car might prove to be unreliable ('no va', Spanish for 'it doesn't work'). This became in my mind the 'no va effect'. Perversely it now seemed a surreal symbol of my life which had simply come to a stop at 'no va'.

Needless to say, not a soul knew about my virtual visits around the world. So I lay there totally silent and motionless, frozen in a kind of hibernation.

My rather sardonic sense of humour often saw the grotesque side of my predicament. I even reminded myself of El Cid, or at least Charlton Heston's final incarnation of him, in his last battle, galloping out of the gates of Valencia to face the Moors in all his finery. Even before they had strapped him to his horse, he was in fact long dead.

—— CATHERINE ——

Facing an Unbearable Truth

People keep asking me where Hasso finds his courage each hour, each day. I find the question surprising. Perhaps because if they knew him well enough they would never have to ask.

But how am I to answer them? His family, of course, has never been a stranger to the need for courage. I know, for example, what his grandfather has always meant to him. Though Hasso never knew him, he knew enough from what his father told of that one dark day in 1938 to feel immense admiration for his courage. He has told me about him many times and I can't help thinking of those stories as I try to imagine how it feels to be in Hasso's position right now.

In the 1930s Hasso's grandfather was working as a *Landrat*, a kind of District Commissioner, in Schlossberg, East Prussia. During the night of 9 November, the infamous Kristallnacht, he faced what was, no doubt, one of the hardest decisions of his life. When he received orders that he was not to intervene in the destruction planned for the synagogue in his district, he knew that he had reached a crossroads of conscience. He had long been at odds with the regime and was deeply disturbed by the mounting persecution of Jews and other minorities in the vindictive climate of Nazi Germany. Another Bredow, an implacable opponent of Hitler, had already been murdered during the Night of the Long Knives in 1934 when the purge against Röhm was used as an excuse to liquidate prominent officials who were known to oppose the Nazis. Hasso's grandfather knew enough about the system to realise that resistance was not tolerated, but the abhorrence he felt for the growing tide of racism and for the erosion of Jewish civil rights now brought him face to face with a moral imperative. My father-in-law, who was about 16 at the time, remembers how he and his brothers were called in to see him that night, as he had something important to say to them. His father's words were ominous. He was dressed in his uniform and he told them and their mother that he was going to the town to try to prevent one of the greatest crimes against the Jewish people, and that it might mean that they would never see him again. He added that he had made up his mind that this was the only acceptable thing to do. As a 'German and a Christian' he could not stand by and allow such violence to take place; he had to take a stand. Later that night, on the steps of the local synagogue in Schirwindt as the mob raged around him, he stood with his loaded pistol drawn and assured the crowd of Brownshirts and hysterical Nazi faithful that they would only be able to destroy the building over his dead body. Perhaps it was something in his demeanour and his air of authority that made them desist, but the unbelievable result was that the building and people were among the few to be saved that night in Germany.

His actions left an indelible mark on them all, even on the next generation. His story is often quoted by those who seek to understand why it was that others did not follow his example and were unable to find the courage to resist their murderous orders, and also by those who speculate on the fate of Germany had others been willing to do so. Of course, his small victory could not prevent the Holocaust, nor did it do much in the end to protect the local Jewish population from the inevitable flow of events in which they became caught up and in which, ultimately, many, if not most, of them would perish. But for Hasso it has always stood as a kind of moral affirmation of honour. A gesture both hopeless and noble which shows where conviction must be prepared to lead when tested to the extreme. It's a hard act to follow. But I know how it has made Hasso look inside himself and search for the courage to face adversity.

Hasso's own father has not escaped his own personal hardships. Ever since he was wounded in his early twenties, he has suffered disability and disappointment. Hasso's childhood was marked indelibly by this strong and inspiring man. With his limbs severely damaged, he struggled first on two sticks, then on one, and then to his own dismay in later years, once more on two, and finally in a wheelchair. He has always refused to accept the frustration of his limitations and has constantly pushed himself to accomplish the most basic of tasks. He has never allowed his disabilities to become an excuse for not applying himself rigorously to all of life's challenges. All of us have seen him in the garden of his home, sometimes buffeted by wind and rain, balancing on his sticks, determined to plant or weed and refusing to give up until the job was done. There are the sweetest pictures of him with Hasso in the late 1950s; he dark-haired and still good-looking, Hasso small and blond and in awe. One photograph shows him steadying himself on his crutch and forcing his unresponsive legs forward, while leaning down to hold Hasso's two-year-old hand. At times he has been a hard and exacting father, but always loving and fiercely proud of his children. Some of his courage and his steady, tenacious examples have surely left their mark on Hasso. He has loved his father with a mixture of deep emotion and sometimes speechless admiration.

But now it is Hasso's turn to suffer and I know he wants us all to see that he too is made of stern stuff.

However, that's not all there is to Hasso. Deep down there is a vein of even greater resilience that goes beyond the inspiration he feels from such examples. Fundamental to his nature is a solidity that leaves me speechless. I sit day after day, night after night beside him and watch the horrible way in which this condition withers and diminishes his body, but I marvel unceasingly at the strength of his spirit and the firmness of his integrity. He is mute, paralysed into near total immobility and even his facial expressions have gone. But his eyes fix mine with an intensity that is arresting and often breathtaking. Through them I see the wholeness of the unbroken person within. They are the windows onto his inner thoughts and all his pain.

There is something in him that I recognised the day we met, from that first moment even, and that still burns in his eyes with an almost incandescent steadiness. Something quite apart from all the blood that flows through his veins and all the awesome examples of his family history, which in themselves are so difficult to emulate. It's a straightness and a strength. A pure vein of incisive clarity that cuts through the chaos and goes right to the heart of the matter. It was there on the day we first met and I see it still in the intensity of his refusal to give in. He has never been called upon to commit his own act of outstanding bravery or to stand up for his convictions in the face of brutal lawlessness, as his grandfather had to. But, far worse, he is now being tested beyond all frontiers of human endurance. With his characteristic, unbending sense of self and his absolute belief in what holds us together, he faces each moment of each hour with unbelievable dignity.

He has always known what he wants and has never hesitated in deciding what he should do. But nothing could have prepared him for the brutal harshness of this. The relentless, daily attrition of imprisonment within his own body, of the voiceless indignity and the heart-breaking sense of loss. He is denied all means of altering this fate and even his refusal to accept it is ineffective. Powerless spectator that I am, I am unable to control my tears at the sheer monstrosity of it all. And yet, he still finds the courage to continue to embrace that refusal. As I watch him through all the days of his suffering, as I hold his hand and look into those eyes that still have the power to leave me breathless, I see Hasso, enduring and intact, in spite of all that has robbed him of himself.

Swedish Noses and a
Cure for Baldness

The uncomfortable realities of my physical condition now began to strike home with a vengeance. In addition to the basic indignities, there were all the painful aspects of the treatment, which were so hard to bear. The simple, unconscious act of swallowing my own saliva had become a monumental problem and often led me into paroxysm of choking. This was greatly exacerbated by the presence of my tracheostomy which always seemed to be the source of grief one way or another. An inevitable side effect of the trachi, for example, is that secretions regularly build up in your throat and tubes, blocking the trachi itself. Unless these are cleared, it is very difficult to breathe at all, so they have to be suctioned out with a special pump. This involves inserting a flexible, plastic tube into the trachi and pushing it down your throat to 'suck' out the offending secretions. This procedure is actually quite horrible. It is extremely painful and often results in bleeding, which leads to intense soreness. The more it is used, the more it seems to be needed. So there is, inevitably, something of a vicious circle at work. I certainly never got used to it, and always found it very uncomfortable. Although this method is troublesome in itself, however, it was in use a lot on that particular ward. Certain nurses, either through NHS economy drives, or in the misguided belief that it was somehow hygienic, actually tried to wash out the 'Swedish noses' and reuse them. It occurred to me that this could potentially be quite lethal, as it prevents air getting through. It was, in fact, just one example of staff taking the initiative in areas where they had little or no expertise. Whatever the reason, I ended up with a severely blocked airway and moisture dropping down my throat, making me gurgle and choke. I managed to tell Catherine about it and, when she was about to mention it to the staff nurse, she actually saw one individual trying to do the very same thing. After that they were replaced each time it was necessary, and Catherine was given access to a supply purely for my use and learned how to change them herself.

By now, I felt that Catherine had probably saved me from several dangerous and unpleasant situations. Indeed, I began to feel that I needed her there all the time to keep an eye on things and to prevent painful and potentially catastrophic mistakes. She had obviously also realised that this was the case, and this was an additional reason for her spending every single hour of every single day with me. This, however, meant the agonising problem of being away from the children all the time, and only being able to spend time with them during their holidays or at weekends, and then only if they came to the hospital too.

A new development at this stage provided plenty of extra ammunition to my friends and family for teasing me. To my amazement, my hair, which had previously been very thin, began to grow back in patches, the colour actually matching the rest of my hair. Now, I thought, whatever this bloody stroke must mean in clinical terms, it may also contain the cure for balding. This led to a series of madcap schemes from all and sundry for marketing the secret recipe (whatever it may have been) and finally making me that elusive fortune. Not that ideas like these were going to do me much good in my situation. Anyway, not much more than a thin thatch materialised in my case. Joking apart, though, my scalp was just one of the many areas of my body that had developed a kind of hypersensitivity. I reacted with a shudder when my head was touched, or that particular area of my hair was moved. Even a gentle breeze in the outside air would set me going, but that wasn't half as bad as when my hair was stroked, a gesture which, along with holding and stroking my hand, so many affectionate and well-meaning visitors tended to repeat over and over again.

Every day I had a visit from the 'bonebenders' (my name for the physiotherapists). Unfortunately for me, it had never occurred to any of them to agree a sign for pain with me; and although I flashed my eyes at them frequently when the agony shot up above the pain barrier, they would simply carry on with their routine, oblivious. As a result, in response to the pain and in a desperate attempt to attract attention, I started to grind my teeth. This soon grew into a habit, however, or, more accurately, a kind of automatic response which I was unable to control and which will probably prove to be the end of my teeth at this rate.

Apropos of visitors, I was now able to see a few people briefly. My boss and a colleague from the personnel department very kindly came several times, although on many occasions they were unable to see me because I was just too ill. It was a pity that they had to be kept away, as I know I must have missed quite a few visits at this time and I would really have liked to see them. The children came as often as possible and this obviously was not easy for them. Catherine's parents also made the journey up to London to see me as frequently as they could and, in the meantime, looked after the children for us at home all the time.

As for finding distractions to alleviate the tedium of this new life, I was rapidly discovering that all the normal methods were out. I have never been a big television fan but, immobile as I was, I thought it would be a great way of passing the time. The staff agreed that it would be a good thing to encourage me to try and watch some. So, one summer weekend afternoon, I was wheeled up to the ward TV to see the German Grand Prix. I must say, I have always been keen on following the fate of my fellow countrymen in Formula 1 and, in spite of feeling so dreadful, was vaguely interested this time to see how they did. Unfortunately, I was soon to discover that the stroke had so seriously affected my eye muscles that I could not get them into line sufficiently to be able to see the picture properly. This was the first and last attempt to watch any TV for a very long while. It had failed miserably.

Inevitably, this problem also impacted on my ability to read text either on the printed page or on a screen, and I soon discovered that I couldn't really read at all any more. So one of the last remaining comfort zones had also slammed its doors shut on me. Now talking books would have to be the only answer. The trouble was I was now also entirely dependent on someone to switch the cassette or CD player on or off for me.

'As Long as it Takes'

Every day I travel in and out of London, leaving the house in the early morning, often before the children are up and returning late at night, just before or after midnight.

Aware as I am of Hasso's difficulties if I am not there with him to help with communication or even to notice if he is in pain or discomfort, I can't leave him alone in the hospital for too long. The staff, however well meaning they may be, are just too busy to keep an eye open for all the countless things that can go wrong for Hasso in a day, from the excruciating torment of an itch he can't scratch to the agony of intense pain that comes with cramp or as the result of tubes inserted wrongly. To endure such things is bad enough for minutes on end, but when no one is there to notice and a patient is unable through gesture or voice to draw attention to the problem, suffering can be unnecessarily prolonged for hours, even days. For this reason I feel unable to spend long periods away from Hasso. It is bad enough that he has had to endure the long, lonely nights alone, sometimes in a state of dreadful discomfort and even in severe pain. I can't help thinking about him as soon as I leave and waking at night with worries about what might be happening. During the daylight hours I try to be there to prevent the situations that can occur all too often due to the simplest of causes which are often easily and speedily rectifiable. It's frequently just a question, for example, of helping him to shift position, or rescuing him from the inhaler mask which has run out of vapour and would otherwise be pumping dry cold air into him. Sometimes, however, there have been more serious incidents and as a result I have been convinced that it is imperative to be with him for as many hours as I can.

None of this would be possible, however, if I didn't have the most wonderful of parents at home to support me. Though in their seventies and eighties, they have responded to the gravity of our situation with an alacrity and generosity which are as open-ended as they are unconditional. Having moved up from Devon as soon as all this began, they have simply moved into our home and taken over my role with the children and the house. They have no way of knowing how long they will be called upon to keep doing this and have never once asked. They know that I need them now more than I have ever done before in my entire life and they are unselfish and uncomplaining in their willingness to devote themselves to the task in hand. This means, in real terms, all the hard graft of housework and caring for three children whose lives have been shattered by this trauma and whose mother is simply never there to help them through it. They have had to leave behind the comforts of their own home and the company of their friends, not knowing if or when they will return. And they have embraced the challenge with unflinching dedication and love.

Always on hand to do whatever jobs are required of her, my mother gets up with me at the crack of dawn and makes sure I eat breakfast before she takes me to the station to catch the train. Every evening when I step off that train, no matter at what ungodly hour, she is always there to meet me. She keeps dinner for me and fills me in on the news, listening to all the worries and despair I have stored up over the day. My father, as baffled and embittered over the inhumanity of what has happened to Hasso as he is, cannot disguise his profound sense of bewildered sadness. He tries to jolly the children along and to keep busy. He has his regular jobs and helps to ensure that the household keeps ticking over, never once giving thought to his eighty-two years or his own failing health. Confronted with the appalling nature of the suffering they see in the son-in-law they have come to love so deeply, they mourn the loss of his staunch presence and the certainty of his strength. They are speechless in the face of the harsh cruelty of it all. But from somewhere inside they find the dedication and determination each day to continue. All day long they navigate a course through the troubled waters of our fractured family and enable me to spend the precious hours with Hasso.

Week Three

After the rarefied atmosphere of intensive care, life on this ward was to prove very difficult overall. I hated the level of noise and the chaos here and, compared with the nursing I had received in intensive care, there was certainly a very different approach to the patient. This was especially evident in the lack of time for the individual. Moreover, between the dreadful insomnia, so common to brainstem stroke patients, and the constant noise and disturbances from other patients, I was getting quite literally no sleep at all and was feeling terribly low.

This was clearly not an appropriate environment in which to place a severely ill and deeply shocked patient, who was desperately trying to get to grips with the enormity of what had happened. Catherine begged for me to be moved and was told at first that there were no alternatives – I would have to stay where I was. The doctor responsible asked me to give it another shot and finally suggested moving me down the ward to a different bay. The change was, inevitably, purely cosmetic. I was effectively in the same ward, just on a different bay and the same conditions persisted.

Before the move, I had to have a new 'trachi' fitted, this time a size smaller. I was assured that it would be no problem, quick and painless. However, this so-called five-minute procedure proved to be brutally and excruciatingly painful and took about twenty minutes. Unable to scream, squirm or make a sound, I was simply forced to endure this act of barbarity with no anaesthetic and no painkillers. It would not be the only time that, because I could not complain, it was presumed that it was OK to carry out procedures on me, irrespective of whether or not pain actually came into it.

Another peculiarity of my treatment at this time was the use of nebuliser inhaler machines. Let me say that although inhalers may hold a certain kind of fascination for some, that did not mean that I wanted to spend so much time connected up to them. For literally hours every day, I was hooked up to a machine attached over my trachi in order to breathe moist air, which, supposedly, would help to clear the congested airways and stop the rattling in my throat and chest. To be quite honest, I don't think this actually did much good over the year and a half I had to use it. There were also distinct disadvantages to this treatment. Firstly, you get wet all the time with the droplets of moisture dripping onto your face, neck and chest; and then, when you no longer have a trachi and have advanced to mask level, you get an itchy nose all the time ... and, of course, you've guessed it, you can't scratch it. There were so many occasions when the staff left the nebuliser on and then, presumably because they were busy elsewhere, forgot to come back and turn it off. The whole procedure is only supposed to take fifteen to thirty minutes. However, especially at night when Catherine had gone, I was often left for between one and one and a half hours to endure what was, by then, bone-dry air being pumped into me. The effect was far from pleasant.

About this time, life on a crowded, busy ward, where mentally confused patients floated around, causing noise and distress, was leading both of us to breaking point. The fact that no one could tell us how long we would be there or what the outcome of all this would be, together with the physical discomfort and mental anguish we were both experiencing, were rapidly making things unbearable. When I look back now, I realise that breaking point is relative. I had no way of knowing that much worse was to come ... but these were early days. Clearly, however, the situation there was just about as intolerable as it gets, and the worst of it was that we were powerless to get anyone to change things for us. So, yet again, I was expected to endure.

The change, when it came, could not have been achieved in a more lunatic and dramatic way. Even by my standards, it was a pretty spectacular coup, with a kind of 'Pythonesque' quality to it. The upshot of it was, however, that I finally got a double room just for me.

Having been moved along to another bay, I found myself surrounded by several other male patients. In my new row, I kept a close watch on the bay opposite, as it was basically all I could see. One day, the occupant was moved out in the morning. Towards lunchtime, a couple, probably in their late forties, arrived and began to settle themselves in. He was obviously the patient, and I presume that his wife was there to keep him company. They were provided with coffee, which they drank very sedately and then, without a word, proceeded to unpack his few belongings, which they arranged around them very tidily. Catherine and I exchanged amused glances. They must have been quite set in their ways because, without a word to each other, he vigorously started doing a crossword, while she began to tackle her knitting. After a while, a kind nurse offered him some lunch, which he accepted with eagerness and, when it arrived, he set about devouring it with all the desperation of the condemned man who has just been brought his last meal.

Then, suddenly, I had one of my legendary, violent coughing fits, for which I had become so well renowned on the ward. In an uncontrollable explosion of spluttering and spewing, I began to cough alarmingly, 'shooting' the Swedish nose covering my trachea opening (and all its contents) right across the ward. As if watching an action replay in slow motion, I followed its trajectory in horror, as it sailed into the air and descended, with an unpleasant splat, directly onto the poor man's plate, just as he had started to dig in, and thence onto the floor at his feet, splattering his precisely creased trousers in the process. The look of disgust on their faces was priceless. As were everyone's (including Catherine's) efforts to 'mop' up, in a very British way, so that we could all pretend that nothing whatsoever had happened.

Needless to say, while I continued to cough uncontrollably, the curtains were rapidly drawn around my bed, and these also got quite a spraying. Panic began to ensue among the staff. Behind the curtains Catherine endeavoured to replace the Swedish nose and clear up, but was hindered by irrepressible convulsions of laughter and efforts to keep them quiet. Apparently, thanks no doubt to my already lengthy stay in hospital, I was suspected of harbouring some kind of 'superbug' infection and, thanks to this incident, might well have done a very good job of infecting the whole ward in one fell swoop.

A war conference was held among the staff, amid hushed whispers and much to-ing and fro-ing. A rapid decision was made to move me to a side room, probably as an improvised isolation ward. A patient who was due to leave the hospital was moved out to accommodate me, but I couldn't help wondering why on earth we hadn't been offered this solution in the first place. Clearly, I was not to be allowed to consider myself a special case, or to run away with the idea that brainstem stroke with resulting locked-in syndrome was any worse a condition than the various other ailments of the many patients on this ward, although they could still walk, talk, eat, breathe, move around and go to the toilet. Funny, that.

The new room had only two disadvantages, which were, however, far outweighed by the benefits. The first issue was the close vicinity to the kitchen, which meant the noise of cutlery and dishes before and after each meal (not to mention the smell of food you will never be able to eat) provided an on-going and gnawing kind of torment. Secondly, as I had no neighbours, I had been positioned away from the centre of the room towards the window, and visitors often stood on my right side, with disastrous consequences for communication. I needed to see a person's face for the eye alphabet to work properly. In this position, as I could not turn towards the right, it was very hard to see them. It took quite a long time to get the message across, and many of my visitors must have thought that I was actually turning away from them, unwilling to communicate.

Memories

One day an attempt to hoist Hasso into a wheelchair goes horribly wrong. The lurching and swinging motion make him sick and he is returned to bed to be cleaned up. As I sit outside waiting to be let back in a nurse looks up from her notes and comes over to me. She sits down next to me and after a long pause she asks: 'What's Hasso really like? I mean, what was he like before the stroke?' I draw breath to answer but, try as I might, I can't find the words. Not the right words. Where can I begin?

When I close my eyes I see him. Not as I see him when they are open but as my heart sees him. Fragments and shadows.

He sits on a five-barred gate on a warm summer's evening watching the children making daisy chains in the grass. He smiles down at me with the sun in his eyes, squinting into the light. There are lines at the corner of his eyes and grass stains on his jeans.

I see him lying on his back on the living room floor alongside the three children. They are giggling and screaming and are challenging him to a Malteser blowing contest. He takes his time, steadying himself and then he balances a Malteser above his lips, blowing a steady current of air to lift it above his face. He is concentrating all his energy on that one long breath, endeavouring in all seriousness to outperform them. He is so intent on winning, which, needless to say and much to their delight, he does.

In the early evening sunlight he stands there for me on the edge of my memory wearing a leather jacket and shades at the entrance to the hall we hired for Lucia's sixteenth birthday party. At Lucia's insistence he has become a bouncer for the evening, embracing the role with characteristic earnestness. He is checking the guests' invitations and turning away gate-crashers. When the party is in full swing, we share a glass of wine and smile at each other in tacit disbelief that so many years have already passed. He throws back his head and laughs when a sixteen-year-old latecomer tells him he looks 'cool'.

I see his long body folded into an impossibly tiny children's tent on the lawn in the garden next to little Sophia, his legs protruding way beyond the flap. It must be unbelievably uncomfortable. He is pretending to be asleep so that she will follow suit and he can then finally carry her up to bed.

I still see him for an instant when, driving down the village high street, the memory I have of him cuts across the present. He is walking home from the station after his London commute. He is carrying his suit jacket over his arm. His eyes are fixed not on the road, but on a lark high above his head. His tie is loosened, the top button of his shirt undone and his sleeves are rolled up. From the look on his face, you just know that all day he's been longing for this moment.

He's even there in the darkness, as he has always been every year in autumn, holding a child's lantern above his head and leading the children and me through the night-time streets in the old German tradition of the lantern procession. He doesn't care that no one here in England has a clue what we're doing or why, or whether or not they stare at us in amused curiosity as they pass by. He just keeps the children singing the old songs and rhymes over and over again as we walk, so that they can feel the magic of a light in the dark and the defiance of song over the approaching winter silence. The lanterns must have real candles, of course, just like the Christmas tree every year; he hates electric imitations. The children know they look strange but somehow they don't care. They're even proud of it. And he likes that.

There are thousands of pictures, but none will stay. They flit and flicker through my mind.

If I keep my eyes closed long enough there will sometimes come an image of him drinking and laughing with his brother Wichard or friends, cutting wood or smoking the pipe he gave up several years ago but still misses. I can even, with a sudden stab of pleasure, catch in my memory a whiff of the distinctive aroma of the smoke. Occasionally, but ever more rarely, I can almost hear an echo of his voice down the phone line. I find myself holding on long after whoever has been on the line has hung up, listening to the hum of the static silence. Waiting for the familiar tone of his voice in the distance. I hear it, almost, but not quite.

I can see the notes he leaves me and which I find when he's gone to work. I can feel the little quickening of my heart when I discover the small square of paper folded over with my name on it in the most unpredictable of places: under my pillow, in the teapot, in my coat pocket.

I can feel too the imprint it leaves on me, the sullen shadow of discontent I feel when we argue, the way he stubbornly and calmly insists on tiny things, and then, even when I'm in the wrong, calls me from work to put it right.

I see the serious, reflective expression on his face while he listens to someone's problems and then it's his limbs I see as he walks away from me and I watch him from behind, the broad shoulders pulled back and the long, strong legs striding forward with such purpose.

These and thousands of other half-remembered, incomplete and fleeting pictures of him come and go, resisting my attempts to hold them down. I try, but fail to translate them into words. I don't for the life of me know where to start. He's there in all the folds and crevices of my life, my past, my present and my memory. The bitter-sweet taste of all he is to me. Words can't express him.

I look into the nurse's eyes. She can see the struggle in mine. I stutter and hesitate and finally utter the words:

'He was different . . . special . . .'

'Of course,' she replies, with a kind smile. But I know she can't even begin to imagine what I mean. She holds my hand for a brief moment, giving it a tiny squeeze before releasing it, then returns to her work.

When I open my eyes and see him there before me in his wheelchair, the very absence of him burns itself into his physical presence. I want him back. I want the touch of him, the sound of his voice, the sight of him walking towards me. But it's more, much more than that. I feel also his own sense of loss. The pain he feels in losing himself. It's there in every moment and in every look he gives me.

So I close my eyes. And remember.

The Queen's Nose

My wheelchair, when I was well enough to be hoisted into it, was a serious cause for concern. It was realised that this loan chair was not ideal for me, but since I was due to be moved on to another hospital at some indefinite point in time, the staff did not appear to think it was worthwhile doing anything about it while I was still there. The headrest was the main problem. As I couldn't hold my head up, it kept falling in all directions, jerking my neck forwards, backwards or to one side and resulting in sharp pain and discomfort to the trachi. This gave us all a puzzle to solve. I am using one right now with precisely the 'u' shape that my eight-year-old son Christian drew on a piece of paper one day for the staff in an anguished attempt to improve my predicament. The only one available for me to use was flat, with no support to stop my head falling sideways. We really fell in love with this headrest. We were given a headband to tie my head in place, but it never worked properly and, needless to say, I felt terrible with it on. In fact, my wife promised that, when we finally got something better, it would be hopped upon, cut into small pieces and set on fire, because we all hated it so much. It narrowly escaped this fate by going missing one morning. Much to her frustration, she never got to carry out her threat. Eventually, the offending headrest was adapted by the 'bonebenders' when Catherine begged and begged them to come up with something. But when it was in place on my chair I looked like a Longhorn on wheels.

In spite of all these difficulties, Catherine managed to persuade the staff that, after more than two months of never seeing the light of day, I needed to get out of my prison. If we were fortunate enough to get the timing right, and if I was up to it, we were sometimes able to get the wheelchair out of the hospital to the tiny park across the road for a short breath of not-so-fresh London air. The hospital, being in central London, had no grounds of its own, but the park was a pleasant little backwater, well away from the madness of the main streets and actually had some lovely trees to look at. These short visits took an enormous amount of organising. A qualified nurse had to accompany us on every occasion, lugging a full suction machine kit with her in case I began to choke on the spot. This happened a couple of times and attracted not a few stares from onlookers as tubes were thrust down the trachi opening in my throat, and the noisy machine did its work to suction out the offending secretions. The park was a favourite lunchtime meeting place for hospital and office workers, grabbing a quick sandwich and lazing on the grass during their lunch break. I was aware that some found the spectacle less than appetising.

When accompanied by the children on these visits, we must have looked like a motley crew, as blankets, sunshades, sick bowls and mopping-up equipment had to be carried with us each time. We always paused at the entrance to the park for me to decide which end I would like to go to. Contrary to appearances, there was always method behind the madness that seemed to characterise my trips there with my son Christian, whether he came with his sisters, Lucia and Sophia, or with my parents-in-law, as we invariably turned to the right on these occasions. At the end was a large statue of the Queen who had probably given the square its name. This was an interesting part of the park for him. He had quickly discovered that he could climb all over the statue and that the nearby beautiful fig tree provided excellent ammunition for knocking off the ever-present pigeons with surprisingly stinging accuracy from her stony nose.

Although it was agreed that these visits helped as part of my therapy, the fact that they always required a nurse escort meant that they were usually a rarity, and we spent many a weekend hoping to be able to get out into the summer sunshine for a short while, only to be let down time and again.

Outdoors

Hasso loves the outdoors. He loves leaving the city behind him at the end of the day and getting back to the fields and the woods. He's the type who could in all seriousness be quite happy living in a remote, rural location with little contact with the town. He always says that if he had lived in the nineteenth century he would have emigrated to America to take up a frontier existence in Wyoming or Montana, the emptier the better. He always fancied the life of the pioneer; building his own cabin, living off the land, cutting wood and breathing the crisp air of the mountains. It's not just a romantic notion. Given half a chance, I think he might well have tried it if I hadn't come along and the sudden pressing need to provide for a family hadn't made those dreams rather unrealistic. It's a strange irony that, within the same person, a City banker with a flair for finance can coexist alongside a dreamer with a taste for wide-open spaces and the lure of the wilderness.

With Hasso the two have always been there. His childhood was shot through with a wildness that propelled him out of doors at each opportunity and led him to live out fantasies of the Far West in the forests and fields of his youth. With his world punctuated by the myths of the American frontier and raised on a diet of literary westerns (the work of the German writer Karl May seems to be rooted in the fantasies of many of Hasso's generation), his childhood self translated his yearnings for wilderness into his own version of the landscape around his home. With his brother Wichard and close friends he roamed the countryside with home-made bows and arrows, catching fish and small animals and using hunting knives to make dens and dams. Like many boys of his age all over the world, he played out his heroes' destinies in the world of his imagination. And like countless generations of young boys, to him the fantasy often felt more 'real' than the reality. For Hasso in particular, it became almost a metaphor for freedom and an impossibly beautiful, romanticised vision of his lost childhood, resulting in yearnings that have never really left him. The realist and the dreamer wrapped up in one.

As he lies here in this hospital bed there are many things both he and I have to struggle to get used to. I feel the daily, dizzying disorientation, for example, of suddenly being always taller than him now. As I sit beside the bed or push his wheelchair through the hospital corridors, it feels so unreal and disturbingly unnatural to be looking down on his head, when I have looked up into his eyes for so long. I rebel, and resist the realignment. His utter helplessness in all things gives me a further sense of giddiness. I am unable to equate him totally with the strong, staunch man I have shared my life with until now, someone always capable, always in control. But far, far greater than all my bewilderment in the face of this must be Hasso's own inability to square what he feels with what he is. With his thinking brain and his inner spirit untouched by the total meltdown that has obliterated his body, he finds himself imprisoned behind the impenetrable walls that confine him. His love for the forests and the fields and for a certain wild freedom can never change. But now the intoxicating whiff of the outdoors can only tantalise and mock him from beyond the open window.

Six Weeks On: The Downward Spiral

As if things weren't bad enough by this stage, this period is marked in my memory by visions of the onset of all that was to make matters so much worse. Plagued by increasingly violent whole-body spasms, spiralling bursts of temperature and fever, gnawing pain in my limbs, and the agony of all that is dreadful about being 'locked in' with no escape, this period started the slippery slope towards daily deterioration. Due to an underlying infection and the cocktail of drugs I was on (never fully explained to either of us, it has to be said), every day, without fail, I had a visit from the phlebotomists. They were considerate enough to take blood from various different locations, so giving an even, overall bruising effect. They often wore vampire badges on their respective tops and one had a tourniquet decorated with pictures of Dracula and vampires. Humorously meant, but it somehow seemed rather apt to me. In the long term, when I finally moved on from this place, tests showed that I had developed liver problems. It seemed that the various drug treatments I had had which had been intended to target serious infections might have been the cause of this. Frankly, it seemed to me that no one really knew why I was still alive.

I have already mentioned the phenomenon of hyper-sensitivity to touch and, during my time in this ward, I also experienced the sensation of 'super hearing'. I have always had a strange ability to hear the full bandwidth, but at a frequency starting higher. This was in fact only identified in my health check when I did my National Service for the German army. Such acute hearing had often been an advantage to me. I loved, for example, being able to hear bats in the night at the bottom of my garden. Now, however, it turned into another form of torture. I could even hear distant background sounds so intensely that I felt they were right there in the room with me. I could hear patients on the main ward moaning and groaning, telephones going all hours of the day and night, as well as far distant sounds of doors closing and bins banging several floors beneath me. All of these sounds were excessively loud and rasping – and difficult to explain when no one else could hear them. I especially found the constant opening and closing of the lids of the metal pedal bins painfully loud. It was as if all these new, almost tangible sounds were present in my brain like the clearly palpable pulsating and vibrating music one can feel coming from a loudspeaker. At first I felt it was so strange that I wanted everyone to be able to experience what I was hearing, but I soon realised that it was peculiar to me. This would be just yet another example of how my senses had gone haywire as a result of the stroke. This state of affairs went on for quite some time and, although it began to lessen after about a year, even now, the smallest, unexpected sound makes me jerk or jump quite involuntarily out of my skin.

In the face of all these new and disturbing experiences, I was comforted by the presence of some very kind and helpful people on this ward, who even brought some light relief from time to time. One sweet nurse from the Philippines with a heart of gold built up a secret stockpile of hospital gowns especially for me, because, every day when mine needed to be changed, there never seemed to be any available in my size. But the location soon became common knowledge and everybody eventually helped themselves. It wasn't long before they reverted to leaving me wrapped in a sheet, while they went off to search the wards on other floors to find me something suitable. One day, they returned with a small pink floral gown and seemed hurt when I declined it. I indicated that I would rather stick with the shroud. So I did.

For those who find it impossible even to imagine what being 'locked in' is really like, here is a hint: one strange aspect of this existence is that ordinary, mundane objects begin to take on a surreal edge. A lot of time is taken up doing some really exciting things, like staring at the ceiling. This one had many squares in it, out of which my eyes were constantly busy forming crosses. For days and days, I tried to work out what they were reminding me of; then I remembered that, as a young soldier, I had once visited a war cemetery. I was staring at rows and rows of graves.

Not a good omen, I thought.

By now, Catherine and I had well and truly lost confidence in the system. She insisted on staying with me for all the waking hours of the day. The children were being looked after fantastically by her parents, but still it was so hard for all involved, as this was likely to take a very long time to resolve itself.

About this time a terrible thought began to worm its way into my head. The growing spasms and shaking of my hands and feet reminded me too much of the cases of CJD I had seen on the TV. I worried about this for days, before daring to burden Catherine with the thought. She tried to calm me down and to explain again what had really happened, which I actually already knew, but I must have been in such a mentally shocked and sick state that my imagination was running riot. A male nurse had to explain the situation and put me right.

'Right', that is, in the sense that I was beginning to confront the facts, to understand just what kind of horror I was actually dealing with, and to forget about others. From attending the birth of my children, and from having seen the urgency on the faces of the midwives and nurses when things threatened to go wrong, but thankfully didn't, I knew that starving the brain of oxygen is bad news. I was somehow going to have to get my head round the realisation that all my problems stemmed from the death of brain cells. In my case, these had been damaged by the stroke because a clot had prevented blood getting to the brain for long enough to have significant, if not to say catastrophic, results. The very thought was shocking and deeply disturbing, but I had somehow to make myself face up to the fact that it was brain damage that was the crux of the matter, the key to understanding my changed state.

I was beginning to realise that in life the smallest stone thrown into a quiet pond can create the biggest of ripples.

Meanwhile, hospital life went on, against the background of the noises of a busy capital. From my bed I could hear ambulances reversing, wheelie bins, helicopters and sirens filtering in from the outside world. I was still totally unable to sleep at all and had to be happy with the odd hour or so doze per night. In the background, there was always the din of various alarms going off, night staff talking, loud TV sets and telephones ringing. As I was classified as an 'at risk' patient, it was thought prudent for staff to keep an eye on me. They came up with the idea that whoever was on night duty should sit outside my room with the door open. However, no matter how urgent my needs might be during the night (pain, pins and needles, high temperature, choking, etc.) there was nothing at all I could do to make myself heard or noticed, wherever they sat.

After so many weeks, the effects of so much inactivity in my limbs and joints were manifesting themselves daily. Being a complete dead weight and unable to hold my weight to assist the nurses and carers when they had to move me, I had to be 'manhandled' for the slightest thing. Repositioning in bed, dressing, changing sheets, all such procedures had to be done by at least two people – one on either side of the bed – and involved rolling me over many times backwards and forwards to complete one small task. However expert carers may be in this procedure (and some are), the whole thing requires a lot of uncomfortable and sometimes painful man-oeuvring of the patient's body. In my case the constant rolling from side to side had caused my shoulders to pack up, as, more often than not, they simply pulled on my shoulders to haul me over. When lifting up my arms they tended to grab my hands instead of holding the whole arm, causing all the weight to pull on my shoulder joints and wrists. The resulting subluxation has left me with recurring shoulder pain, and this has proved especially acute on my left side, which I cannot move at all, try as I might. The ligaments were basically torn. Defying even the strongest of painkillers, this ache would, from now on, serve as a constant reminder of the new status quo of my existence. So this was what was referred to in hospital jargon as 'manual handling'. Obviously the famous principle of 'Vorsprung durch Technik' seemed to be con-fined to the car industry, or for that matter any other industry that made money. The relentless pursuit of excellence for material gain had obviously not been applied to researching more comfortable, less harmful ways of moving paralysed patients around a hospital bed. Man may be able to walk on the moon, but I would have to put up with being manually hauled from side to side.

There was another major disadvantage to my new state. When I had been moved into a certain position by nurses or carers, I obviously couldn't get out of it. While they were busily chattering about what a great time they had had the night before, or who they had seen in the canteen, I was trussed up into a position which I hated, and which I knew would slowly but surely result in agony. Rapid eye blinks to attract their attention drew little response, and this is entirely understandable, when one remembers that to them, quite obviously, I had more in common with a roll of carpet than a thinking, hearing individual who might be uncomfortable. In their bustling, well-meaning kind of way they would often finish off their task and disappear, leaving me with my legs bent up in bed, cramp spreading rapidly up towards my spine and not a bloody thing I could do about it. By now, I knew that I had lost any control over my muscles, and that it was pointless to will my legs to shift even a millimetre. It would take about twenty minutes for the weight of the upper leg, 'comfortably' resting on the bones of the other one, to become unbearably painful. Lying like this is OK when you can adjust your position; otherwise you have to endure the pain and wait for help. At night this often meant that I'd have to wait till morning when Catherine came to rescue me. A night spent like this can be excruciatingly long, and it can feel at times as if tomorrow will never come.

Doctor's Visit

Frustration and intense fury smoulder away within me. The unsuspecting target of my rage at the moment are those Hasso calls the 'Gods in White', the team of doctors and students led by a senior doctor who do the rounds of the wards. I suppose my anger needs some kind of outlet and they are the people who seem to be most frequently on the receiving end right now. Not that they would know, though. I strive to preserve courtesy and politeness in my manner when they descend, but there are increasingly frequent moments recently when these begin to show signs of fraying at the edges. I just can't help it.

One of the major sources of frustration in hospital life is the infrequency, and total unpredictability, of the doctors' rounds. On the other hand, everything seems to revolve around these consultations when the senior doctor and his team arrive to pronounce on the progress (or lack of it) of each patient. And their importance, sadly, cannot be downgraded in relation to the scale of disappointment they engender.

Since Hasso was admitted to hospital the pattern of these visits hasn't changed much. In fact, after an initial short-lived flurry of interest in his case in the first few weeks, I have sensed a weary indifference developing ever since. I suspect that the very absence of real progress in Hasso has resulted in a decline of active involvement in his case. Of course, I have to remind myself that it's not personal. But I'm not sure that that doesn't even make it worse, since the depersonalisation of everything in this medical nightmare is contributing to my sense of outrage and causing a real distortion in my relations with certain members of staff. Admittedly, I can imagine that after weeks of stalemate in one patient's progress towards recovery, it is not inconceivable that attention wanes in favour of those patients who respond to treatment and promise the satisfaction of a successful outcome. The truth is, though, that I cannot but rage against this show of what I feel to be off-handed indifference. I am finding it impossible to accept, even from a purely scientific point of view (given the rare nature of such strokes), that the medical team is not more enthused by Hasso's case or motivated to monitor and strive for an improvement in his condition. It just doesn't make sense to me. Instead, the apparent lack of concern on their behalf stings in exact proportion to the frequency with which it is displayed.

Standing next to Hasso's bed, the doctor addresses him for the umpteenth time with the same series of inappropriate questions; questions which have been asked over and over again since day one.

'Can you make a fist?'

'No,' blinks Hasso.

'No,' he has to repeat when the doctor finally looks up, surprised at the silence that has greeted his question.

'No,' I repeat aloud for his benefit and in an effort to remind him politely that Hasso can't answer his sodding question, although in fact he was here the day before, and the day before that, and the day before that, and should remember that Hasso can't speak.

'Can you open your mouth?'

'No.'

The eyes peer over the half lenses of the glasses perched on his nose, the head not bothering to move.

'Can you wiggle your toes?'

'No.'

I look down at Hasso and see the weary look of disappointed admission. The questions rain down like hammer blows on his already fragile attempt to muster his courage in the face of growing despair.

'He can't do any of that,' I offer, ignoring the withering look from over the glasses. 'But he can move his thumb a little and he has even managed to move his leg off the bed a few centimetres a couple of times.'

I try to keep the tone positive. I want them to pay attention to anything that Hasso can actually do. I desperately need them to acknowledge the small steps towards what I want Hasso to believe is progress, anything that will make him feel a tiny smidgen of success. Why on earth don't they ask what he *can* do rather than what he can't?

The spectacles glance in my direction as if a troublesome fly had landed on his nose. He ignores my contribution and, with a mild trace of irritation, proceeds to address the students and the junior doctor in tow. The words are mumbled and incomprehensible. I haven't understood a thing and I know that Hasso won't have either.

Undeterred, and emboldened by the feeling of anger beginning to rise now in my throat, I try another angle. Careful to keep the fury out of my voice, I am, however, conscious that the polite smile I greeted them with has now left my lips.

'I know those things aren't on your checklist,' I begin, the choice of the word intentional though perhaps unwise, 'but surely the fact that Hasso can do those things, however tiny they may be, is significant. Especially ...' I add, as the spectacles turn an irritated upward glance towards me, 'especially as he ... he couldn't do them last week.' My voice trails off.

It sounds pleading and faintly pathetic. This isn't going well.

An awkward silence ensues. He coughs a dry little cough and adjusts his tie. 'I'm afraid not,' he replies, addressing me directly this time. 'Totally useless, you see. He can't rely on these movements, or do anything with them like clean his teeth or feed himself. So no, they're not significant.'

The fish eyes stare up at me across the rim of the glasses and I could happily open my mouth and scream at the top of my voice until the men in white coats come and take me away. Scream and scream until all the anger and frustration spill out in the manner of a perpetual version of Munch's 'Scream'. My head is seething. I'm capable all of a sudden for the first time in my life of doing real violence. I feel that I hate this man with a passion I didn't know I was capable of. It is his use of the third person that really gets me and the total ice-cold unconcern for the effect of his words on Hasso. Each and every one falls as a deep laceration. The articulation of all that Hasso dreads and fears, the reduction of his whole sense of self right down to nil. Only this man can't even have the decency to address them to Hasso himself.

I stare ahead at what to me at that moment looks like cold indifference and feel myself teetering on the edge. My fingers are hot and twitching and my temples are throbbing. I can feel it coming. Then, all of a sudden, before I explode, he swiftly gathers up his papers, and without a word, sails off to the next bed, his cowed entourage holding up the rear. The junior doctor gives me an embarrassed and mildly sympathetic look as he turns and follows behind.

I hold onto the rail at the side of the bed and try to steady myself. I'm aware that Hasso is looking at me intensely. I try to slow my breathing and take my eyes off the back of the suit that is retreating down the ward.

A cheery nurse comes up and suggests that they get Hasso ready for his physio session. Unable to meet Hasso's eyes,

I take the chance and tell him that I am going to get a cup of tea but will be back when he's up in the chair to wheel him down to physio.

Outside the door to Hasso's room, I take a deep breath and wait a moment until I can focus properly. A few feet away is the door to the stairwell. I walk firmly towards it and dive into the gloomy deserted space behind the door. Only then do I burst into tears.

Bonebenders and ATDs

If I was up to it, I was visited in the mornings by a team of physios, usually two, who took me through a routine of stretches to prevent my limbs from tightening up altogether. On most days, unless I was really ill, I was also taken in my wheelchair to the hospital gym for a session with the 'bonebenders'. I was hoisted onto various pieces of equipment and exercised for about forty minutes. I often found this quite tiring and frequently became very dizzy. All the residues of strength and fitness that had taken me years to build up had all too rapidly succumbed to the withering effects of my condition.

When I returned from my daily session at the gym, a therapist from the speech and language department was usually waiting around for me. Apart from a strange tendency for them all to be called Sarah (a fact, in the case of all my speech therapists then and now), they all repeatedly tried to perform the so-called 'blue dye test' on me. This test was designed to show whether or not it would be safe to work towards removing the trachi, or even introducing some pulped food at some point. The key thing is whether or not your swallowing mechanism is reliable enough to prevent food and liquids being aspirated into your lungs. Blue food colouring is squirted into your mouth for you to swallow as best you can. If any of it ends up in the trachi, then it proves that you are in danger of aspiration, and no further steps are taken. In spite of repeated attempts to perform the test on me, I always seemed to fail it. They also had a series of exercises that they wanted to run through with me, involving sticks and ice cubes to stimulate the tongue.

The lack of any serious progress on this front seemed to disturb only me. In spite of the absence of improvement, they just continued with the routine. For a long while, my teeth remained firmly clenched and I couldn't open my mouth one iota. If it could be prised open a few centimetres, any slight touch would make it snap closed instantly, injuring any helpful fingers which happened to be in it at the time. This was a state of affairs that Catherine rapidly discovered to her peril, when she was trying to clean my teeth. On the other hand, the after-effects of a major stroke are perverse in the extreme. Totally unable to get my mouth to open at will, I was, however, becoming famous for what I called a 'mega' yawn. My mouth would open like an enormous cavern when I yawned, completely involuntarily, and then snap shut again. This kind of contradiction was becoming part of the way my life was developing. I also seemed unable to control the only two sorts of emotional reaction left to me. Quite unnervingly, I would laugh at things that were totally unfunny, or descend into a flood of sobs and tears which I was unable to stop. I am told that this condition is strikingly common in stroke victims, but it is still deeply disturbing to those experiencing it.

Various different devices were employed at this time to counteract the relentless progress of nature's decline in me. To the amusement of my children, I had to wear tight white stockings. These fetching ATDs, as I dubbed them (anti-thrombosis devices), also came in pink, but I managed to resist that temptation, so white was the only option. My family seemed to find it irresistibly funny to see a man's legs in white tights. By the time the so-called 'economy-class syndrome'

(DVT) hit the news in a big way, these stockings would thankfully have reached their sell-by date with me. By then, my legs had become so thin, the nurses kept having to find ever smaller sizes for me (which were always too short for my long legs or too small for my long feet) and, finally, they simply had to give up using them.

My general discomfort was now exacerbated by the much dreaded pressure sores, which had started to form in some places, in spite of my air mattress. Strangely enough, one such problem area was on my ear, probably because I had been left lying on my side for a long time, with my ear bent forwards. As a pressure relief device, a rubber glove was blown up, or filled with water, and slid between ear and pillow. This, too, provoked uncontrollable laughter from my children who likened it to a cow's udder. Needless to say, the udder proved to be pretty hopeless at surviving any visits from my adventurous children.

Routine

There is a routine even in this hospital world. Of course, it's someone else's routine and it revolves around a whole set of unknown patterns and rules which one slowly acquires. At the very beginning it's like entering an alien environment and one's instinct is to want out as soon as possible. When that is not an option, one learns to pay attention to the signposts and signals in order to make some sense of things. Little by little, a grudging but intimate knowledge of this new world begins to evolve.

This is important. Months on end in one circumscribed space mean that one's brain needs to understand the structure of the institution in order to preserve one's own sanity. This probably also applies to other places like boarding schools and prisons, as well as to hospitals. You learn to work out who to talk to in order to get things done, who to side-step and who to humour. You learn the mundane rhythms of the hospital ward and its idiosyncratic timescale. You become acquainted with the demon tedium and how to deceive yourself into thinking that you can win the relentless struggle in keeping him at bay. You learn also that, no matter how empathetic certain members of staff are, this is still just a job for them. They are not part of your personal tragedy and the truth is that, unlike you, they can all go home at the end of the day to that world, now so detached, but to which you also once belonged.

And you never quite lose that awful sense of guilt. Guilt that you have spent an entire life up to this point, never thinking, never even dreaming of the intense suffering that goes on each and every day in the bodies, lives and minds within these interminable hospital wards and corridors all over the country and all over the world. The extremely sick and disabled up and down the land, effectively incarcerated in their own world of frailty, pain and despair, travel the difficult road of their personal life's journey; and we do not see them. It is as if they inhabit some kind of parallel universe just outside our sphere, yet lying very close. When, on those very rare occasions, these worlds collide, as they have done for us, the shock of the discovery is unnerving and unsettling. And the guilt floods in. Why have I never seen, never known, never chosen to know before this that such suffering exists?

The longer you stay in this environment, it becomes an experience of extreme disorientation to attempt to reconcile the two worlds. Essentially that is what I have to learn to do each and every day and it perhaps explains the bewildering sense of dislocation I feel all the time. In this place I exist alongside Hasso and he is the one and only parameter of my world. And above all, I devote most of the day to the time-honoured crusade of killing time for him. Distraction is all. Reading aloud, talking to him, encouraging him to spell out his thoughts so I can write them down. I desperately try to keep his mind and spirit from falling into the vast, bitter expanse of despair that washes round his bedside and which all too often seeps between the sheets. Sometimes I feel rather like some demented shepherd keeping the wolves of despair at bay with the sticks and stones of mere words. Anything not to let the beasts in. We both know how awful things are. To name them or speak of them is simply too painful.

When I leave here each evening I walk through the London streets in a kind of bemused trance. It's like gliding through some virtual world. Why, I can't help thinking, do the people drinking, chatting and laughing not realise that life has stopped? How can they embrace, tell jokes, carry shopping, catch the bus, all as if everything is so normal? How can the whole world carry on as if nothing has happened, when such horror lies just beyond the walls of the very buildings they walk by? But, of course, it is precisely the same life I too was living until just a very short time ago. Now I have to force myself each day to engage in these 'normal' activities. I must return home each night to my children and parents, I must buy train tickets, make phone calls, book a service for my car, pay the electric bill.

Real life, though, seems to have acquired the solidity of air, to have transformed itself into the insubstantial quality of paper.

Outside these windows it feels as if collective amnesia has blanketed the world. Crowds sleepwalk past the horror, forgetting that we too at any moment may slip through the black hole just below our feet and find ourselves immobile and mute on a hospital bed where the door has closed and there is no way back.

Distraction is all.

The Bedroom Jury

There was a dedicated 'stroke nurse', who was not supposed to come and visit me because her work was mostly with conventional stroke patients with good prospects of recovery. She had, however, already visited me in ITU and remembered me, so occasionally she would steal some time and come up and see me. It was always a pleasure to see her, and she had the most intense eyes I have ever seen. She was like a breath of fresh air. It was good not to be talked down to and to have someone who would listen to me, even if this required all the patience and time necessary to follow my eye blinks and spell out the words letter by letter. Moreover, she had the courage to ask the hardest of all possible questions about how I felt about life, about death and about continuing. However, there remained one unanswered question between us. She explained that she felt that Catherine should not come every day, all day; that the strain would prove too much and that she should take a whole day off every week. I could not and would not give her that one day per week. I couldn't bear the prospect of a whole day without her. I really needed her to be with me. In fact, at this stage I seriously treasured every single moment because I knew we might not have much longer together. She must have suggested the same thing to Catherine and, although Catherine never mentioned it, I know what her response must have been, because she never spent a single day away from me during the whole year I was in hospital.

There was also an English nurse of Irish descent who was truly like an angel to me. I liked having her around, as she was the kindest and most skilled of all the staff on the ward. She did everything she could for me. Indeed, I liked to think there was something of the 'hand of God' in the way she looked after me. She was also a great support to Catherine, who, when I was so very ill, was often there all night when this nurse was on duty. But, however good individual members of staff were, they could do nothing to affect the outcome of things when they were not around. In other words, in such a difficult situation, even with the best will in the world, one good person can't make an awful lot of difference. You are simply fighting a losing battle. Although I did come across some unsung heroes during my time in hospital whom I have never forgotten, and who did so much to brighten my dark days and nights, it has to be said that they were very definitely in the minority. Incidentally, this nurse was the only one who, some time after we had left that hospital, actually made contact with us later to see how I was. I remember being very touched by that.

However, under-staffing is a chronic problem in our hospitals and its effects were very apparent to us. The lack of permanent staff, particularly in London, means that many slots are filled by 'bank' or agency personnel. It was not easy to get used to the constantly changing agency staff. Handovers sometimes took on the character of a rather comical farce. Every day, a verbal synopsis of each individual's case was presented to new staff at the foot of the patient's bed. This usually turned into a case of the blind leading the blind, as even the departing nurses didn't seem to know the patients they were discussing. To speed matters up it appeared easier to shortcut procedures completely. Consequently many mistakes were made.

Although perhaps unintentional, what to me seemed clear errors of judgement and sheer incompetence became an almost daily occurrence and we began to dread the unknown dangers of each new day. Here are the results of the bedroom jury. I will leave the allocation of points, however, to you.

My trachi was a major area of point-scoring here. For example, the application of nebulisers without removing the 'Swedish nose' became a common occurrence, basically because many agency staff had never seen one before.

One of my favourites for the 'nursing cock-up of the year award' was one that none of the perpetrators ever seemed to notice themselves … the elbow versus trachi competition. Needless to say, I always found myself on the losing side of this one, as each day brought a new tally of how often staff could knock, nudge, jar or pull on the trachi tube sticking out of my throat. Being unable to shout in pain, and somehow almost invisible to staff as a result, no one even noticed the tears welling up in my eyes when it happened. On the pain scale, it certainly scored pretty high.

Another hot contender was my bath routine. Because the hospital possessed no shower trolley (a kind of plastic-covered bed on wheels on which the patient can be showered), I was told that bed baths would have to suffice. As a two-shower-a-day man, I felt unspeakably awful after several weeks of this, and Catherine had to plead and plead with staff to offer some alternative. The best they could come up with was stripping me naked, hoisting me onto my wheelchair, draping a sheet over me and transferring me to the bathroom down the corridor, where I was hoisted naked into the bath, washed and hoisted out again to do the whole thing in reverse. Some staff seemed to compete with each other for how long they could leave me dripping wet in the chair and one actually returned me to my room and walked away. When asked by Catherine if she would be back soon to dry and dress me, she looked rather surprised at this. 'Does he want to be dried too?' came the question. Amazing. An unusual request, or just me being awkward?

Perhaps even hotter on the jury's list might be the almost daily occurrence of being left suspended in mid-air, sometimes virtually naked and often dripping wet, because the electric hoist (that wonderful 'crane for humans') had run out of juice. Someone (funny, no one ever seemed to know who) had forgotten to leave it on charge.

Another favourite contender has to be mentioned here as, for many of my friends, it really is the front-runner. Although I had plenty of practice at it, I was never able to get used to breathing under water. Unlike the character in Otfried Preussler's book *Der Kleine Wassermann*, I was most unsuited to the dangers of deep water. My bath was a valuable and treasured part of my routine, but the actual process could be a bit hair-raising, to say the least. The staff entrusted with this task at the beginning were very competent and the whole operation usually involved about four, sometimes five, people as well as Catherine, who was there lending a hand every time. There were obvious dangers in lowering a patient with a tracheostomy into a bath full of water, not least of which was the possibility of water entering the trachi tube and flooding the lungs. As time went on, and my bath-time became part of the routine, the skilled staff involved began to delegate the task to ever more incompetent and unskilled people. The result was inevitable. Once, I was lowered into the bath with my trachi tube wide open. Catherine's alarm stemmed from the stunned realisation that, I would, in a matter of seconds, have a lungful of bath water. She thought that they must surely know what they were doing, and would obviously be aware of the impending danger. Her shock made her shout out an instinctive warning. This immediately made her feel embarrassed, but was actually enough to save me on that occasion. She was learning to take nothing for granted and to realise that she had to be vigilant all the time. The burden this entailed was clearly immense.

Unbelievably, even when the water was kept at chest level, hoisting me in and out often caused a sudden lurch forward and this was a bit hairy at times. In addition, care was hardly ever taken to avoid water splashing and lapping up into and over the 'Swedish nose' when it was left on, which left me coughing and spluttering on many occasions. It is sadly true to say that there were only a couple of members of staff with whom I felt safe and who were capable of performing this and other tricky tasks with sufficient care and skill. Unfortunately they were rarely around when these things had to be done.

Once, while Catherine was off preparing the bath for me, I had the pleasure of a bumpy hoist ride directly from my bed to the bathroom, which was quite a way along the corridor from my room, because the care assistants had forgotten that I was supposed to be transported in the wheelchair. Taking me to the bathroom in the wheelchair was not only intended to be for the sake of comfort, but also represented a nod in the direction of some kind of dignity. The lack of both of these was rammed home to me on this occasion, as I was actually naked, draped only in a sheet, swinging about in the hoist.

Whatever the results of the 'bedroom jury' may turn out to be, the struggle to protect me from incompetent, unfeeling and unkind staff (most of whom, it has to be said, were from various agencies and not part of the ward staff) came to a head one day when two events precipitated things to a new height. One morning Catherine arrived to find a large puddle of urine on the floor. On checking, she discovered that the catheter was leaking. It was immediately obvious that no one had attended to me during the night or they would have noticed the leak, which had also soaked my bed and had overflowed onto the floor. How could this kind of treatment be possible? There was, however, worse to come.

Soon afterwards, Catherine arrived as normal in the morning, only to discover what, in the half-light of the still darkened room, looked like a repeat performance. Looking more closely, however, she realised with cold horror that it was not urine, but blood. Trying to keep calm, she ran to find a nurse and finally returned with a kind and sympathetic ward sister who, thankfully, was on duty that morning. It turned out that an agency nurse had been in charge of the ward over-night (as I was well aware) and at around one in the morning had come in to give me medication and check on me. I had been slightly alarmed at how rough she was, but was not prepared for the shock when, in an offhand way, she somehow yanked on the catheter tube. The pain was excruciating. I knew something awful had happened. I waited in vain for someone to return in the hope that the damage would be noticed. Until Catherine arrived the next morning, however, waiting was all I could do. The prison of silence and inertia is sometimes worse than just tragic. I was to pay dearly for this incident.

During the following days, the passing of urine hurt intensely. In addition, full body spasms began to contort my body each time my bladder opened. This is now a feature of my daily life and something that I have had to bear ever since. A doctor from the urology department came to examine me and pronounced he hadn't come across a case like this one ever before. It would not be until later, when I entered rehab, that I got an explanation for it. For the moment, however, this was the beginning of the worst phase for me since the stroke.

Sure enough, I began to develop a fever. Within days a UTI (urinary tract infection) had set in and I was seriously ill for months afterwards. With my immune system already seriously depleted, this opened the door for a series of spiralling infections and I knew now that I was becoming desperately ill. Antibiotics didn't help much and I slipped further and further downhill. I was no longer able to sit in the wheelchair and my visits to physio were stopped.

A tiny flicker of movement in my right hand, which had given us such hope that a recovery might be setting in, retreated and then disappeared. Much later, some of this returned, but, despite two years of physio and many desperate efforts to improve on it, this is still confined to my right hand and my right arm up to the elbow.

I remained in bed all the time, very feverish, losing weight rapidly because I couldn't tolerate any of the artificial liquid feed any more, and getting weaker by the day. Catherine sat by my bed all day and, increasingly now, most nights. I think we both knew that it was probably only a matter of time. I seemed to be too weak to be able to turn the corner. Certainly, as days turned into weeks, the doctors and nurses seemed to have given up hope. Everyone now just seemed to be waiting.

Through the nightmare of fever and pain, I slipped in and out of consciousness. My spirits were very low, but from time to time a light would sometimes penetrate my darkness. Over the head of my bed was a sort of console covering the strip lights and this had become full of cards, messages and pictures from well-wishers, family and friends. They were from all over the world, from the past and the present alike, going back some thirty years. There was just one period missing. Lying there in the twilight of the here and now, suspended but not released, I lingered in a sort of half-life where memories of my childhood and youth, in particular, kept recurring. My best friend from that time had been a very special person to me. We had drifted apart over the years and I had no idea what had happened to him. For some reason, though, I often thought about him in this nether world, as fragments of remembered days in the fields and woods, playing bow and arrow or hunting for mushrooms filtered through my consciousness. Later, an event quite unexpected by me would bring all these memories flooding back even more clearly. For now, however, I simply thought about him a lot and remembered life as it had once been, an eternity ago.

Smile

I love his smile. There's almost nothing I love more about him. Except perhaps his laugh. Yes, maybe his laugh has the edge. Everyone I know loves to hear him laugh. But seeing his smile and that special way he has of catching my eye and winking at me still makes my heart miss a beat.

Months have passed now and I am seriously beginning to wonder if I'll ever see that near magic look as his smile creases into being and his laughter begins to ripple in infectious, life-affirming waves. He seems to have travelled off, to somewhere so very remote that I can't reach him. Can it be that he will not make it back? This monstrous possibility is beginning to occupy most of my waking thoughts. The realisation that he may not merely have slipped into this altered and inaccessible state for a short while, only to re-emerge fully himself again, but that he may never come out of this is slowly but remorselessly insinuating itself into my mind, despite all my efforts to keep it out. It floods me with panic and disbelief.

But something makes me force myself to contemplate the reality of the almost complete lack of any real progress. And it terrifies me. I wait and wait and wait. Rather than edging forwards to the light and to recovery, he seems to be slipping back further and further into the deep, dark chasm of immobility.

I miss his smile and his laughter. Probably because they are so much a part of him. And he is unimaginable without them. Of course, he can't smile at all now. Not really. Since the stroke, he has been unable to summon enough control of his face muscles to enable even a flicker of a smile to cross his face. Sometimes his face contorts a bit and something resembling a smile appears. But it's not his smile. And occasionally he does laugh. But it's not his laugh. I've discovered the odd nature of the difference between voluntary and involuntary muscle movement. Smiling and laughing are no exception. It seems at times that some stranger, some unknown, uninvited outsider has taken possession of his face. Twisting it and pulling it into unnerving counterfeits of his smile and his laugh. He doesn't look like himself now when he smiles.

And something awful is beginning to happen. I can't remember his laugh. His real laugh. I try so hard to picture him telling some stupid joke and throwing his head back as the laughter takes over. I focus all my memory and attention on recreating that deeply endearing smile in my head, so that I can feel I haven't lost him completely and I can still believe that he will return to me; but I can't. And it breaks me that I can't. Some days I feel like all the edges are melting away. Things fall apart and the very shape of the familiar and the well loved is crumbling from the outside. How can I lose hold of something so fundamental as the memory of his laugh?

The Twilight Zone

The constant fever, combined with the way the stroke had affected my body temperature, now resulted in a shivering chill that seemed to envelop me completely, although the thermometer showed my temperature to be constantly around 40°C. I have always had cold feet at the best of times and always jokingly blamed that on their distance from my heart – my central heating, as I liked to call it. But this reminded me of the all-embracing cold I had experienced during the German winters of my military service. During exercises, we were often required to sleep on the snow in just a sleeping bag, covered by our 'Dachshund garage', which is what we called the small army tents we used. Being an artillery man, my only (literally) cold comfort was the so-called 'soldier's bride', a heavy machine gun that I had to keep in my sleeping bag with me to prevent it from jamming with the cold. At least then I was not the only one feeling the cold.

In addition, by now my weight was down to 68 kg, a figure I had last reached before I did my apprenticeship at my first bank some twenty years before. That meant that I had lost 23 kg in little over six weeks. The effect was awesome. I felt it was certainly a bit sudden for the old pump; that was, after all, a loss of around a quarter of my total body weight. There was nothing I could do about it. I could only lie there and feel myself fade away.

With the growing weakness came an overwhelming and constant dizziness, regardless of whether I was in bed or seated in the wheelchair. Whenever I was moved, turned on the bed, or hoisted, it took about an hour to get my centre of gravity back . . . and that can drag on quite a bit. I would lie or sit there trying to fight down the nausea and light-headedness, while things went on around me in a spinning haze. It occurred to me, on more than one occasion, that there was a certain irony in all of this: some people actually pay good money for drug-induced sensations like this, while I was getting more than I had bargained for – totally for free.

During my time in the army, while doing my bit to maintain peace and security for NATO and the German government, or so we were told, I was twice based near AF Cent (Allied Forces Centre) in Holland. It was there that I first became exposed to drug-taking on a serious scale, and I discovered quite quickly that I was in the somewhat uncomfortable minority of people who were just not interested in doing drugs. What it did to my friends on a regular basis would have been enough to put me off, but the scrapes we tended to get into when we were all out together during off-duty hours certainly helped to keep me away from the stuff. There were several rival groups in the town, all busily fighting each other on most nights, and drugs and alcohol tended to exacerbate the conflict. There were, of course, the native Dutch; then there were the descendants of various ethnic communities from the former Dutch colonies around Java, including two groups of girls; there were also the local Rockers, dressed in black leather with the name of their clubs on their sleeveless jeans tops, and three groups of soldiers – Dutch with their 'obligatory' long hair, Americans in crewcuts (known to us as the 'Korea battle-cut') and Germans with very short hair. Finally, there were the waiters from the bars and discotheques, where all groups regularly seemed to meet.

Drugs were readily available. With the benefit of hindsight, it's not difficult to see that this combination was a recipe for disaster. It certainly didn't take long before most of the groups were at each other's throats. The fact that each group was so easily identifiable tended to escalate the tension. The waiters, who were dressed in long green aprons, protected themselves and their premises with wooden truncheons like baseball bats. Whenever there was trouble, they would wield these menacingly, and often laid into the more troublesome elements with gusto. I saw them in action more than once. Whenever we found ourselves in the thick of things, the only thing we could think of was to leg it as fast as possible. It was time to find a nice unmanned border crossing in the woods and get back to the shelter of the barracks.

Somehow I had never envied my friends' ability to get themselves high on whatever substances turned them on. Ironically enough, here I was now getting it all for free. Indeed, I was soon to experience my own 'trip' of such epic proportions that it would have awed any of my former comrades. Going on the experience of the last trachi change and all the pain involved, when the time came to replace it again I got Catherine to tell the doctor that I would prefer to be put out during the procedure. The doctor showed considerable surprise at this and assured us that the procedure was painless. This time, however, we were not going to be duped. Catherine seriously urged him to do something to get me out of it for a while, so that they could do the job without me suffering so much pain. Reluctantly, he agreed and asked the nurse to bring morphine, but I was rapidly to discover that the desired relief was not to materialise and would turn all too quickly to horror. The morphine injection was given, and, without giving it a moment to work or have any effect, he immediately proceeded with removing the trachi, whipping one plastic tube out of my throat and slipping another in. Just like that. The pain was searing and sickening. Blood spewed everywhere. The morphine only began to take effect half an hour or so later. Far from sinking into the arms of sleep, I was plunged into a 'horror' trip that lasted for hours, but which felt like two days. This time I repeatedly saw vivid visions of cockroaches, graves and images of myself being buried. These continued to roll before me like some manic cinema screen even when my eyes were wide open. This was a very distressing time – both for me and for Catherine. She had to watch me hyperventilating, pinned to the bed amid soundless screams, as I was bombarded by the pictures in front of me. It was horrifyingly real and it was, I must confess, a welcome release when it finally retreated.

When I looked back on this experience a few days later, I decided it had been a very good thing, not just for me, but in the interests of national security, that I had stayed off the stuff in my youth.

Reaching the Edge

For a while, for quite a long while, he still looked so good. It was astonishing. In fact, it took a few weeks to detect the first big changes. When Hasso's sisters Oda and Daisy came to the hospital for a few days back in May, just after he had had the stroke, they both remarked on how good he looked, lying there in the bed. Seeing his strong face and firm body, his good looks still intact, it was so hard to believe at first glance that this terrible thing could actually have happened to him. Until, of course, one registered the total absence of movement and saw him being moved around by others.

Nevertheless, despite his strong constitution, Hasso's body, like anyone else's, had its limits and when the stroke began to take its toll, its forward march became inexorable.

Now it is high summer. Outside, the London parks fill with the chatter of the young and eager and happy. Unseen by Hasso lying in this hospital ward, the leaves have unfolded and fill the branches of the lovely trees. Birds have grown from tiny helpless creatures into miracles of flight. And through all this time Hasso has been fighting a silent, losing battle.

He has lost twenty-three kilos, more than three and a half stone, in less than three months. His face is drawn and ashen. Despite the daily physio sessions, his limbs have gone from being sturdy muscle packs to wasted, bony appendages, hanging or lying uselessly on the bed. His body is thin and lifeless, racked constantly by sharp, rigid spasms. His hair has turned slightly grey and, although he has little or no control over the movement of his head, it has developed a strong pull to the side. It tends to lock at an angle, despite all our efforts to release it. Day by day he has weakened, shrunk and melted from me. There are times when I have felt almost like knocking furiously at the invisible wall surrounding him and shouting, 'Where are you?'

There are other times when the pain of it overwhelms him and he can't stop the tears or the way his whole body gives vent to a desperate loud wail of despair. He doesn't want people to hear it, but he has even lost control over the ability to conceal his emotions and is often unable to stop the sobs and the piercingly desperate keening that accompanies them.

As the year has blossomed into sweet, harmonious summer, Hasso has sunk deeper into this nightmare. When the doctors told me at the beginning of all this that he would more than likely die or, failing that, that he would be weak and ill for a long while and then eventually die, I refused to believe it. They did offer the tiny possibility that he might make a partial or even full recovery, but hastened to add that that was highly unlikely.

Perhaps Hasso foresaw a final possibility even then, the alternative that I have struggled all this time to deny. Surely, if his mind has come to rest on the thought that nothing will ever change, then this is more awful to him than anything. Of course, the doctors in all their deliberations with us never mentioned that. What they have done on a few fleeting occasions is to hint obliquely that Hasso himself might have begun to contemplate the future like this and that he can't face the agony of it. They have even suggested that this appalling struggle will only end when he lets go. His body, certainly, has its limits and it is glaringly obvious to all of us that he has reached them now. But his spirit is so strong. It has been so resilient all these months and hasn't wanted to let go.

Until now.

At any rate, that's what I am beginning to detect in him. It feels like a sort of closing down of the shutters like a slow, silent lowering of the lamps. When the children came to see him today, he seemed to ache with sadness. I had resolved to prepare them for what I have been told could happen any day. They can see how weak he is and I tried to tell them that the doctors don't think he can survive. But how, in God's name, do you find the words to tell your children that? I vowed to find the courage to tell them straight, but found myself slipping and sliding round the enormity of the task. Looking into their eyes, I felt the words tangle and the truth begin to slither away. I was utterly unable to articulate the simple words themselves. The silent, stubborn appeal in their lost and unbelieving faces stopped my lips and dried my throat.

But I needn't have tried so hard. Hasso's face and eyes today told them more than I ever could have. Christian had been saving up a precious piece of news for him. Desperate to hold onto the man he has idolised all his life, he gazed down at him and saw what his eight-year-old heart had never wanted to see. He managed in a strangled voice to tell him: 'Pappi, I got a strike at bowling the other day . . . And I love you very much, you're the best Pappi in the world.'

Hasso continued to look into his eyes, a tired, far-away look, the pleasure of it hurting perhaps even more than the pain.

He is now so ill, I find it hard to understand how he can go on like this from day to day. He is vomiting on and off all the time, his body has been invaded by a fever which has kept his temperature at about 40° C for weeks and his cold, clammy limbs run with sweat day and night. Today one of his doctors gave uncharacteristic vent to his feelings of impotence and horror. Struggling to control his emotion, he said that what Hasso is experiencing is an 'insult to life', and he doubted that Hasso wanted to live.

Although he is conscious all the time and never seems to sleep, he avoids my eyes now and only rarely tries to spell things out.

It's true that deep within him I sense a yearning for it all to end. I see that now. Finally. I can feel it brimming up in his silent tears and bursting out of his weak and unresponsive body. It all but shouts at me in the silence. It is a voice that begs for my acknowledgement, grasps me by the hand and pleads with me to listen. For weeks and weeks I have had my hands over my ears, have denied it my full attention, have refused it place in my fragile, crumbling world. But now, with his eyes staring into the empty space before him, that steady unerring gaze, the silent voice has become deafening to my ears.

It is so strange, but, momentous as this realisation is, I find myself also facing it with nothing but silence. It's almost as though, having come this far together, there is nothing left to say. There are no words for this, the biggest of moments. Suddenly the world has become almost totally silent. As I watch Hasso breathe, I hold his hand and stroke his face. I feel the weak pulse in his wrist. There are no words left. Only waiting. Waiting.

And yet, and yet ... There was unutterable sadness in Hasso's eyes today when the children gathered round him, hugging his lifeless body and telling him how much they love him. But beyond that, undeniably, something deeper, something as yet unwithered. The children's words echo in my head. Christian's defiant attempt to cheer him, Sophia hugging him and squeezing his hand, telling him she misses him. Lucia leaning over to kiss him and whisper something in his ear. They claim him as their father now and forever, no matter what happens.

Something tells me the doctors and nurses are wrong about his will. There is no peaceful resignation there. There is only struggle and implacable resistance. 'Surviving is so hard,' he spelt out a few days ago.

Perhaps there is a gnawing need in him for this to end. But I know too that, whatever comes, he will not go willingly.

Beyond the Twilight Zone

The loss of all my strength and the recurring infections had left me hanging on by a thin thread. This was a state of affairs that the hospital didn't really know how to cope with. I was desperately ill, probably nearer to death than I realised, but what everyone seemed to be waiting for just never seemed to come. I was slowly realising that there was to be no simple way out for me.

I obviously couldn't stay on at a hospital where no one could think of what to do with me, and the search began to find me a place in rehab. The choice was to prove easier than we initially thought. Of the three hospitals on offer, my favourite option was one very near to home, but this one was soon eliminated from the picture because they would not take anyone with a trachi. Of the remainder, the selection was really made for me through the restraints of a waiting list. I did not want to wait a further seven months in hospital to get into rehab, so it was down to a choice of one. I was told, however, that it could take an indeterminate period of time to get in there, maybe even another three months. At that rate, given the present state of affairs, I didn't know if I would even be able to hold on that long, let alone what shape I'd be in by the time a bed became available. So the waiting game continued.

The wait for this bed would have been a good opportunity

to see family, friends and colleagues, but sickness had put a spanner in the works, and I was too ill to benefit properly from all the visitors I had during this period. My brother and sisters came for short visits at this time, but things continued to look bleak, and I could tell that they found these visits as hard as I did. The journey never seemed to bother them though. Catherine and I had often joked that we Germans seemed to be rather addicted to travelling. As a nation, we seemed to be unable to kick the habit. I have often been teased by British friends and colleagues about leaving towels on deckchairs, and upsetting more than the balance of payments wherever we tend to go.

One visit that was obviously long overdue and was perhaps the most painful, but the one most wished for, was that of my parents, who had as yet not seen me at all since my stroke. The situation was not without its complications, as my father himself is seriously disabled and has been since the war. From his early twenties, when he contracted polio, he has struggled with withered limbs and, until recently, had to walk with crutches, until he was forced into a wheelchair by a stroke on his remaining 'good' side. My mother is now my father's main carer and is far from being in the best of health herself. As a result they had left it to their envoys, my brother and two sisters, to come to England to visit me. In addition, I had felt that it would be better for my parents to postpone a visit to me until I was in rehab and, hopefully, beginning a recovery, and they both agreed with this. Now, however, my condition had worsened to such a point that I began to wonder whether I would actually ever see them again.

Sunday

The walls are uniform magnolia. The floors, a clinical blue. It's hard not to notice the floors. After all, I spend hours staring at them, in the same way, no doubt, as Hasso has been studying the ceilings and all their hues and patterns. There are occasional stray clumps of dust under the bed, like fine confused tumbleweed. The walls were once smooth and clean but former patients have left the scars of cards and photographs long since removed. The children have tried to cover them up with ours. Flecks of green show through the bits they have yet to patch. Something inside me wants them never to cover all the flecks. The longer someone stays in this place, the more the wall gets covered with mementoes of home and their former life. The real pros have made their little corner look just like a greetings card shop. It reminds me of being a student and trying to make a cell-like rabbit hutch into something more like home. I don't want this wall ever to look like home. I want someone to rewind the tape and put us all into reverse. For the whole thing not to be happening at all. Edit, undo.

Except it is happening and I have a hunch those little green flecks will all too soon no longer be visible.

The afternoon is warm. The air hangs heavy with chemical odours. Not exactly unpleasant, but definitely smells I have only ever smelt in hospital. It's Sunday. The worst day. Time cloys, drips slowly. Nothing ever happens on a Sunday in hospital. No doctors come, no therapists visit, nothing disrupts the solid block of hanging time. Some patients have visitors in the afternoon, but today no one will come for us. The children spent all day here yesterday. Saturdays are only marginally better than Sundays on the tedium scale. For Hasso, it means that there might be enough staff on duty to wheedle a trip into the park outside. Fifteen minutes of sunlight and summer sky in the middle of the teeming city, thirty if he's really lucky. But Sundays are a no-hoper. Saturdays are also when visitors might come. At the beginning it was always a day when someone or even several people came. Time passes and people don't come as often.

He always longs to have the children here and when they come they stay all day. I watch his face as he listens to their stories and their animated attempts to make him laugh. For all their efforts, I know that he can see the strain behind their smiles and hear the sadness in their laughter. But he never lets them know. They spend hours and hours with him. He loves it when they're here, but deep down he feels they shouldn't be. This place is hardly the best environment for them. He'd much rather imagine them doing the normal things kids do, seeing their friends, going out, laughing. What they haven't told him is that they also feel the same. The odd pull in both directions: hardly bearing to spend a day without seeing him, yet hating this place and everything about his condition that keeps him here. He feels that outside there's a world they should be re-engaging in, one that perhaps can comfort them a little, or distract them ... perhaps. At all events, Mum and Dad will be trying hard today to normalise their weekend life as much as they can. But I know that inevitably they will think about him during the day and will try to swallow the lump that constricts the throat when they do.

Hasso's brief trips out in the wheelchair to the park are a major enterprise, as he is not allowed to go anywhere without a nurse, in case his trachi blocks (as it often does) and he needs to have it cleared with special suction. It's a serious undertaking even though the park is only twenty-five yards from the entrance to the hospital. But it's worth fighting for. Just to see the breeze trace its gentle course across his face and ruffle his hair a little. To see him close his eyes and drift for a moment into remembrance.

But today a trip would be out of the question anyway. He's been so ill for days now that all attempts even to get him out of bed into the wheelchair have been abandoned. His condition has deteriorated so seriously that he is barely able to endure more than a few minutes in it. He is weak and depressed and fever and pain make everything unbearable. Each day merges into another and, with nothing to break the monotony, it's difficult to tell the difference between them.

Something significant in him has changed. Something fundamental. It's not hard to see that he has recently become much weaker. That's clear, but what is going on in his heart and mind is what worries me. He seems to have slipped for now way beyond my reach. I try again and again to rally him, but he seems exhausted. His eyes are the only real door into his inner mind. Although he can open and close them, he finds it hard to control the direction they move in. He tries, but they judder and rebel. Today they seem to float, resolutely drifting away from mine. Today, I know, is a bad day. Probably a very bad day.

He's in a side room now, on his own. In the distance I can hear the clatter of the lunch things being cleared away. I'm glad he is no longer surrounded by the sights and sounds of other people's food, now that he can't eat a thing and hasn't done for months. It seems a cliché to say he loves food. Everyone loves food. But Hasso *really* loves food, all kinds of food; the taste of it, the smell of it, the whole ceremony and celebration of it. And I know how hard he finds it to have even that pleasure denied. Sometimes I can feel the gnawing of his desire when he sees others eating and watches them obliviously enjoying a meal. In here, even the far-off sound of patients being served an insipid hospital meal has been enough to make him almost imperceptibly narrow his eyes, in Hasso a sure sign of pain, the tiniest shadow of a sea of accumulated disappointment and grief.

But not today. His temperature is up again, his face is drained and pallid. It seems that he isn't even really aware of what's going on beyond those doors today. He wants, instead, to be a million miles away. He wants no conversation, no reading, none of my usual attempts to distract him. He closes his eyes from time to time, but I know he isn't sleeping. When he opens them they seem focused on somewhere very far off. The windows are wide open in the warmth of the afternoon. Between us, silence. Beyond, a myriad of city sounds floating into the room and life being lived by countless others. In here, fathomless stillness. I feel a sense of unremitting absence, a sort of continual ebbing away.

I sit in the armchair beside the bed. I hold his hand as it lies on the white sheet through which I can feel the sinews of his once firm and muscled leg. I lean my head against the hard back of the chair. I watch the veins in the back of his hand and occasionally stroke along the length of his long fingers. They are limp and strangely cool, given the level of his fever. They are damp and they leave a cold trace on the skin of my fingers. The curtains at the windows lift gently and fall back on the occasional breeze.

A memory lifts with them. His hand taking mine and threading my arm through his. Walking me along the empty road past the fields of long, swaying rye and barley, he talks incessantly. Another place, another time, a thousand years ago. He is animated and he tells me over and over how happy he is, how beautiful it is to have each other, how wonderful it is to be alive. In the air, the warm dry scent of dusty grain. He talks of the children we will have, of the life to come. We walk right to the edge of the woods in the glow of a sun setting low in the sky. Looking back, we can just about see over the undulating sea of pale green wisps towards the little house at the end of the village that was our home for those first three years.

I truly thought at that moment, and at so many moments after that, that it was impossible to be happier. It's a feeling that stayed with me for so many years, that suffused every day of my life right up until the day when the world seemed to split apart.

If I close my eyes now, I can just about feel the gentleness of the breeze from the window on my face and it floods me with the memory of that other time. It doesn't seem so long ago, that moment of pure contentment, and all the other yesterdays before today. Not really. It feels so close sometimes that I almost believe I could reach out and touch it. I want to keep it all before my eyes, every moment. Yet there are times now when I can only face the day and all it demands if I keep the memories and the knowledge of him firmly locked away. In a place where they cannot overwhelm and drown me. But despite my efforts they often lap so very close and will not be resisted. Today the softness of the breeze has let them in.

His eyes drift slowly towards mine. He has been thinking too. Remembering. I can tell. But as usual the sweetness of the memory is bitter. He's forced himself back to confront the now. I smile at him. For a moment his eyes rest upon mine. Pale, limpid blue, much paler than they ever used to be. They look into mine and the silence hangs between us. I smile again. Not much of a smile, but in it a world of emotion.

For a moment his eyes linger. Then they drift away.

This is a bad day.

Beyond Caring

The long wait for transfer to rehab continued. When a date was finally decided on, I had been in my twilight zone for eighty-five days. My departure also coincided with a total refurbishment of the ward I was on. In the week preceding my last day, the ward discharged all of its patients and accepted no new ones, so that I was the only patient left on the ward. Early one morning, about five days before I was due to leave, the demolition men arrived and started pulling the main part of the ward to bits. My side room became like an island in the middle of a demolition site. By now, however, I was too ill to care much. Catherine and my sister spent the last few days and nights of this existence with me, waiting anxiously beside my bed. I suppose everyone thought that I would finally just slip away.

I spent the last two nights in a side room of another ward, looked after by my Irish nurse, who had volunteered to see it through with me. I don't think many people thought that I would actually make it to the day of transfer, especially as I took a serious turn for the worse on the last day. I had slipped into a constant round of vomiting virtually every hour and was hardly conscious any more. As if this wasn't enough, it was decided that my trachi would have to be changed again, just one hour before my departure. The inevitable trauma. However, the sedation I had been given for the journey actually helped with the pain a little this time, but, by the time I was ready to leave, and the ambulance pulled away towards West London, I was beyond caring what the outcome would be.

PART THREE

As Good as it Gets

July 2000 to March 2001

Shock

As I get down from the ambulance while Hasso is being lifted out on a trolley, I look up at the huge facade of the imposing Victorian building we have come to. I see that the large letters announcing the name of the hospital have been mounted directly onto the same space that displayed its previous name. The bold letters proclaiming 'Hospital for Incurables' are, however, still clearly visible beneath the new sign. A watery feeling invades my stomach and I place myself in front of Hasso as they lower him out of the ambulance, hoping that he won't catch sight of the words.

The first sight of the main building is a shock that leaves me reeling and bemused. Built on an elevated site in an area that was then outside London, the original house had been constructed as a hunting lodge. It is grand and imposing, with spacious landscaped grounds that are indeed a welcome sight after the cramped and busy streets of central London. Having been extended to accommodate several new wings, it is a sprawling edifice which seems to swallow us up. The high walls and the interminably long corridors leave me feeling disorientated. Some areas of the building stun me with their elegance and beauty. The entrance hall is gracious and the ceilings in places generously stuccoed. The floors are marble, there are elaborate brass handles on the doors and polished wood is everywhere. We pass what looks like a stunning ballroom with fine French doors which would not disgrace a period château. I catch sight of an imposing library complete with a breath-taking ceiling. I am simultaneously bewildered and charmed.

Here every single one of the patients is deeply and dev-astatingly brain injured. Many patients here will never leave their beds. Few can communicate in intelligible speech and, but for the odd groans and shrieks, most are silent. Many lie in alarmingly twisted shapes, some gesticulating wildly, others stone-like and horrifyingly still.

I am finding it hard to stop shaking. The warmth and kindness of the staff who greet us wash right around and over me. There is an insistent singing in my ears and my chest feels tight; the voices around me sound very far away and I catch myself staring back at the smiling faces with what must look like bemused panic.

I know that Hasso's arrival here should be the beginning of a new stage and that to have managed to get a place on this rehabilitation programme is the very best chance he has left. Indeed, the reputation of this place for being one of the premier locations nationwide for neurorehabilitation makes Hasso's position deeply enviable. If he has any chance at all of making significant progress, he will find it here. But my heart is thumping and it feels like something very important, something fundamental is seeping out of me. My brain refuses to catch up with and embrace what is going on around me.

Here, each person's humanity has been reduced down and down until it can be reduced no further. It is indeed to this place we have come, and no other.

In a dizzying, shattering moment the world tilts and loses its kilter. The oxygen of hope has finally run out. I look inside myself and feel only the vertigo of freefall.

A Rethink

In effect, the initial period in this new hospital began in the same way as the old one had ended. Basically, most of the time I was as sick as a parrot. As a result, I was kept on a diet of water only, since I couldn't keep anything else down, and my weight continued to plummet.

The first few weeks were spent trying to get me stable, as no real rehabilitation therapy could get under way until I was out of the danger zone and, at the very least, the sickness and diarrhoea had halted and my temperature had come down. With great care and skill, my new doctor worked with the nurses and dieticians towards this goal for the better part of a month. However, I had brought with me from the other hospital a drug regime as long as your arm, which, apart from the water, now formed the only constituent of my diet. It was becoming increasingly obvious that it would be necessary to have a closer look at my cocktail of medication, particularly as this had already resulted in a certain amount of liver damage. Little by little, most of the drugs were withdrawn. My new doctor, whom I teasingly called my Goddess in White, quickly realised what was wrong. In addition to the serious infection, the damage to my brain had also resulted in a state akin to seasickness, where all movement and the attempts of my juddering, unstable eyes to take in the world around me resulted in extreme nausea, which actually made me physically sick on many occasions. Slowly, in spite of several setbacks, things started to stabilise and I began to emerge from the shadows. A new feed regime was gradually introduced and I eventually stopped being sick.

My overall condition, however, had not changed at all. I was still inert, unable to utter a sound or swallow properly, and I was still reliant on my trachi tube for breathing and eye blinks for all communication.

Now that things had begun to level out, the first problem for me to solve in this new place was to ascertain the cause of the full body spasms, which have continued to rack me daily ever since. So far, all queries to the various doctors on this point had brought no answer whatsoever. My new doctor, however, explained that my brain could no longer isolate the commands to my body, so, whenever involuntary muscle movement was set in motion (yawning, passing water, etc.), instead of the required individual muscles going into action, my whole body would contort and tighten up for between thirty and sixty seconds. While this didn't actually hurt so much, it was extremely unpleasant.

I was now getting to know this new doctor and was beginning to discover that she was like no other doctor I had met before or since. She has had such a deep influence on me and has continued to support and help us as a family, long after all her professional obligations to us had ceased. We are proud now to be able to call her a great family friend. To say that she is a unique kind of person is putting it mildly in the extreme. She has enormous depths of compassion and a deliciously wicked sense of humour, and she is herself also in a wheelchair. Her wheelchair driving skills were legendary in this large hospital of long corridors and big corners. She had mastered the art of driving around corners pretty much on the outside two wheels of her chair, and could be seen almost anywhere in the hospital, flying along at breakneck speed, faster than anyone else could walk or even run, rather like an escaped Formula 1 test driver. This often reminded me of the speedway races I used to attend as a bachelor on my 750cc, and I really admired the way she managed to pull this off without skidding. Next step up could be a wheelie, I thought, with amusement.

The move to this place was to signal many changes for us. The hospital was situated beside a slow-moving dual carriagewaay on the one side and lovely, descending parkland on the other. Formerly a private residence, it had been bought in the middle of the nineteenth century to use as a hospital. Catherine was allowed to use the car park and, because she could now drive there and back each day, this meant we would have more time together. The building nestled elegantly into a hill and what seemed ground level from one side was the first floor on the other. We were to spend a whole nine months here, only the time it takes for a baby to be born, but which for me felt like an entire lifetime.

As the symptoms of the critical condition that had pushed me right to the edge slowly retreated over the next few months, it was here that it finally dawned on me with real clarity that I was going to survive. I began to realise that for now there was to be no bowing out for me. Death, with all its terrors and the full weight of its sorrow, had long seemed preferable; but I began to see that life, with all its unimaginable pain, was what I was left with, whether I liked it or not. I tried to focus once again on life and to concentrate all my efforts on resisting depression and trying to think positively. Indeed, at this stage it was beginning to seem that I might even get to take a second bite at the cherry. After all, who could tell what the ensuing months would bring in terms of recovery? That little pipe hanging out of my stomach and the trachi in my throat acted as my lifelines, and they would see to it that the curtain would not yet fall. So it was that, for now at least, I had avoided my confrontation with Cerberus.

Trees

Outside Hasso's window in the parkland that surrounds the hospital is a beautiful maple tree. If I turn his head towards it he can see its branches and watch the sun coming through its canopy. He can even see the wind lift its lovely leaves. He has always loved trees. He loves them with a strange intensity, a kind of earthy respect, bordering on veneration. One of the first things he told me when we met was how upset he had been when all the oak trees in his village had been cut down to widen the road and make way for traffic. He had been appalled at what seemed to him an act of pure vandalism. He had taken pictures of the oaks so he could remember them forever. He still has those photographs, I've seen them many times. He was about ten years old at the time.

He has always said that if he could have chosen a profession in life he'd have preferred to have become a forester. His brother-in-law has a forest in Bavaria and he's always dreamed of swapping the City for a life like that. Strange for a banker! Recently his plan has been to buy a small patch of woodland and look after the trees. He loves the feel of wood and the warmth of the grain.

There's a lot about Hasso that reminds me of trees. Constant, strong and generous. A haven and a shelter. Solid and dependable. I can't help remembering that when we first met he had been cutting down a tree that had just about come to the end of its life. In its place he had planted another. Each house we have lived in has been named after the most prominent tree in the garden. There have always been trees at the centre of things for Hasso. I'm glad that in this place there are so many trees and that he can see them each day. He can watch the late summer turning now to autumn and trace the passage of time as the leaves fade from green to golden brown, and finally fall in the stormy gusts of wind. Perhaps he will see the spring coming forth in buds and blossom and it will give him courage and comfort. And even a little peace.

Rehab

I often joked that there should have been a sign on the door of my new ward reading 'Swahili spoken here', as this pan-African language seemed to reflect the make-up of most of the experienced team on this ward. I really enjoyed the colourful speech and behaviour of my new carers and nurses who proved to be among the best and most caring people I have ever met.

Meanwhile, routine rehab life grabbed hold of me with a vengeance, and daily sessions were gradually dominating the order of the day again. There was a battalion of various therapists from all different disciplines. They were allotted sessions with each patient every day, so that we all ended up with an individual timetable. There were the occupational therapists (OTs), with a sort of overall interest in various areas, from helping patients with dressing and eating, to supervising wheelchairs, splints and communicative technology – the former of which, of course, they could not do with me, and the latter for which I tended to see a great deal of them. Then there were the speech and language people, whose major preoccupation with me seemed to be determined attempts to get me to swallow minuscule portions of yoghurt in order to stimulate my swallow. I couldn't help being reminded of an episode in Roman history concerning a king called Jugurtha whose name always made me think of yoghurt. I vaguely remembered that Rome had had to send an army against him and had fought a long and difficult campaign. He was known for his cunning and his violence and my battle with the tiny mouthfuls of yoghurt became a daily struggle which to me had distinct parallels. As I couldn't control my swallowing muscles it made me cough and splutter and often ended in my struggling to breathe when it slipped down the wrong way. Rome had eventually crushed Jughurta, but since the speech therapists thought the technique useful and showed no sign of changing their strategy, I had no choice but to continue to fight it out with the yoghurt pot on a daily basis.

Then, of course, there were the bonebenders, the IT staff and last but by no means least, the psychotherapists. The latter were by far and away my favourites. I used to smile at their alternative title of 'psychoterrorists' until, that is, they got stuck into my case. The trouble was that they always managed to pose the most inappropriate and uncomfortable questions to which, in my position, there really were no meaningful answers. 'Are you any happier today than you were yesterday?' or 'How would you rate your mood on a scale of one to ten?' It was always a wonder to me that people could study and train for so long and occupy such elevated positions in the medical world, and yet appear to have so little feeling for the people they actually worked with. Although they doubtless believe they have the patient's real interest at heart, it seemed to me that their one really obvious qualification was their ability to practise the art of stating the perfectly obvious. How about: 'This must be a really difficult experience to deal with' or 'Life has changed a lot for you' for starters? Has it never occurred to such people that, never having been touched by tragedy themselves, they are singularly unable and unequipped to imagine one iota of how it actually feels to have one's life left in ruins? That, rather than listen to their insensitive monologues, or be forced to answer their wincingly painful and prying questions, you would much rather be able to lift your foot with just enough strength to be able to boot them as far as possible down those long corridors, and right off the face of your painfully restricted little world. Their earnestly well-meaning demeanour, together with a bearing that implied they possessed the only kind and helpful way to handle such a delicate situation, just added to the sense of frustration and horror I felt.

In their wisdom, the hospital management believed the input of the psychotherapists to be so beneficial to patients that I was allotted a full four sessions per week. Oh joy! As it became increasingly obvious that these sessions were causing me more distress than any possible benefit, Catherine asked for them to be removed from my programme. I never regretted that, but it was sad to see the distress it caused to some other patients, who, sadly, had no one to speak up for them.

1 *September 2000*

We sit together in the gardens behind the hospital, Hasso in his wheelchair, me on a bench. I am holding his hand. It is a day of sweet sunshine and Indian summer warmth. A day also of memories, but they are those we cannot bear to speak of. I know, though, that we are both thinking the same thoughts, sharing the same remembrances.

1 September 1982, the day we first met, was also one of glorious late summer. It is the only anniversary we have ever really kept. My family had come together for the wedding of my brother and his German fiancé and were staying with her parents. A few days before the wedding everyone got together for the traditional *Polterabend*, an informal party held for friends and family. As Hasso was a neighbour and old friend, he came striding into the garden to meet us and to discuss arrangements for the ceremony. I had never seen him before but it was a meeting that would come to be etched on my memory in crystal-clear detail.

It was very warm, but a gentle breeze was stroking the grass and lifting the leaves in the afternoon stillness. Beyond the garden stretched huge flat fields and the village languished under a blanket of slowly ebbing heat.

We were all sitting on the terrace having tea when he joined us. I could guess from everyone's reaction at his sudden appearance that he was immensely popular with the family.

He sat down with us and immediately assumed the centre of everyone's attention with an ease and a bearing that I had never seen in anyone before. It was at once arresting and modest. A kind of natural, inborn grace. With his long legs stretched out in front of him, his jeans and polo shirt dirty from cutting down a tree, he told us, in his nearby garden, he leaned back to shade his eyes a little from the sun. It looked as if the work had been strenuous. He appeared to be hot and tired, but he was relaxed and seemed at ease with the world. He immediately launched into conversation with everyone but me. His English, though halting and imperfect, was more than good enough to charm my whole family. I glanced at him from time to time, affecting a casual indifference, but I can remember feeling distinctly light-headed.

He already knew my brother quite well and teased him about the coming event. I was surprised that he could be so spontaneous and laid-back in a foreign language. Although it was clearly not so easy for him to find the right words as quickly as he would have liked, this didn't seem to bother him. As he chatted, I sometimes caught his eye and found myself quickly looking away. I felt mildly irritated at my own coy reaction, and tried to make myself hold his gaze. I remember feeling my pulse race and my breathing quicken. But he continued with his chatter apparently, it seemed, oblivious to me. I noticed that his arms were tanned with the sun and his eyes seemed to smile at each person he spoke to. He engaged everyone in the group in the conversation, but to me he spoke not one word. Not once.

I was bewildered and confused. I thought he simply hadn't noticed me and found myself nursing a latent disappointment. I couldn't have been more wrong.

When he got up to leave, he politely wished everyone goodbye until the party before the wedding that evening. And then it happened. He turned to me and looked right at me.

His gaze lingered for a moment and I saw the opal blue colour of his eyes. He waited a split second and then he smiled at me. Not a word, just a smile. It was the most direct, the loveliest and the most memorable smile I had ever been gifted. It hung there in the early evening warmth between us and held within it more meaning than any words could have mustered. His whole body was still and in that instant, as he looked at me, I saw an honesty and an undisguised tenderness that utterly disarmed me. I was stunned and speechless.

No one else seemed to have noticed it, but to me the shock of it was complete. I felt dazed yet strangely calm. Then he turned away.

As I watched him walk away into the shadow of the garden, I barely heard the comments spoken in the now vacant imprint he had left in the warmth of the still afternoon air.

But, convinced that I had just experienced something that had changed my life, I kept the smile, and what I hardly dared to imagine it meant, to myself.

Late Summer 2000

I was considered to be so ill when I arrived at the new hospital that I was given a room for four all to myself. It wasn't equipped with an alarm bell, but, considering that I was unable to press the button anyway, it didn't matter.

Long hours of inactivity and immobility have a curious effect on the brain. My habit of ceiling-gazing now had a new object of interest. This one was covered with a curious kind of what I liked to call 'photo-wallpaper', full of what appeared to me to be handwriting. My son told me that he had seen exactly the same kind of ceilings in his school, so I reckoned it must be standard for public buildings. During the hours I found myself indulging my new hobby, I felt a strange sense of recognition creeping over me. What did my sore little eyes see here? The more I stared, the more I felt that I knew exactly whose hand had left this jumble of initials. In a weird moment of déjà vu, I recognised thousands of my own squiggled initials all over the ceiling, the very ones I had used to sign off thousands of reports and documents over the years. As I have often heard preached at many business seminars, it is always useful to have a very different business signature from the one you use privately. The same applies to the initials you use for verifying faxes to indicate whether you are dealing with an original or a copy. Over the years of working in banking, much of it before the PC conquered offices around the globe and when we still had to use the services of a typing pool for reports, I had developed a method for initialling documents to sign off their authenticity. As I had to be so wary of typing errors in documents submitted to me by the typists, rather than just ticking them off I usually initialled every single one. Now, in the depths of this new alienation, right there above my head, sprawled across the ceiling in a tangled mess, I saw my very own initials, duplicated thousands of times.

The longer I stared at the ceiling, the more I began to recognise the writhing mass of apparently random squiggles. In a surreal moment of the familiar, I saw the handwriting of several former colleagues and even recognised the signature of a head of department who used to sit opposite me in my office several years before. His characteristically pointed initials were unmistakable. Then the whole surface began to shift into a bizarre kind of clarity. Suddenly, lifted from the chaos of the random, as if the encrypted had suddenly become transparent to the code-breaker, there emerged on that ceiling masses of text and notes all annotated in this man's inimitable style, complete with remarks in the margins, mainly in German, but with small comments in English, long since forgotten. I remember wondering in a strange flash of lucidity how on earth all that had got there. To everyone else they would just look like random squiggles which, of course, they were. I was aware of that. But for a while, the dream had pushed through the boundaries of reality and it was more than a little unnerving when the moment had passed. There was, however, something about the experience that was emblematic of the world in which I found myself, where the grotesque and the surreal had conquered and pushed aside all normal, decent boundaries of existence. The metamorphosis was engulfing my whole world.

My new reality was stranger than fiction.

The hours I spent staring at the ceiling became, in fact, a metaphor for my new state of being and, as such, grew ever more deeply disturbing. This was obviously a serious shift for someone who, at work and at home, was known for his practical bent, who was relied upon to be clear-thinking, well organised and calm. In fact, I could usually be sure of finding most bits of information quite quickly, as I had developed a pretty disciplined way of recording and organising them. Now all this kind of information has become largely irrelevant, and personal details have had to be confined to memory.

At about this time another serious problem began to become more obvious to the staff here, namely that my vision had indeed been severely affected by the stroke. I heard them discussing what I had actually known all along. I was unable to see properly at all any more. There hadn't really been a great change in the acuity of my sight, but the eye muscles had been damaged to such an extent that my eyes were constantly juddering and I couldn't move them towards the right field of vision beyond the mid-line. This was actually the side of my lazy eye, which has been a niggling problem since childhood, but which, until this moment, I had never really noticed that much. Now I knew why I had had all those pencil-size torches shone into my eyes by various nurses in my first hospital. Not being able to see in a straight line or to let my eyes travel from left to right meant, of course, that I couldn't read anything, couldn't watch TV, or, at this point, see enough of a computer screen to benefit from any of the technology on offer. In my position, those activities would have been a good way of passing the time, but it was to be months before I was able to watch TV or look at a computer screen without extreme discomfort.

Improvement with my eyes was very slow and there were several peculiarities about my vision now. I could not see falling raindrops in the air any more. However, I could make out the unmistakable evidence of rain on the wet ground. I could follow the news on TV if I could concentrate on a static person reading it. Obviously, it was any kind of movement that presented a problem, in addition to all the other issues, as I could no longer focus on rapidly moving pictures. It did not necessarily help that my left eyelid, the worse of the two, was obstructing my vision, as it was very sluggish and slow to open and close. That actually improved a little over time, until the problem finally disappeared in the summer of 2001.

Books still remained out of reach, though. Due to my inability to control the eye muscles enough to scan text from left to right across a page, even if the book was held right in front of my field of vision, I was unable to read any writing. Reading would certainly have been a great comfort, since I could now do nothing else, and I must admit that I miss it a great deal. Even trying to read text on a computer screen is almost impossible without increasing the font to a ridiculous size. So I have had to surrender that pleasure along with all the others.

However, although I have never been able to see a television screen properly since my stroke, I slowly began to be able to watch the screen without suffering dreadful nausea and this was to mark a significant departure for me. One day, on the way back from the library, Catherine caught me trying to follow the picture on the TV in the common room and realised that, for the first time since the stroke, I was actually able to see and follow something of the picture on the screen. After that, I began to watch TV more often and this inevitably helped to kill some of the dead hospital hours. I still couldn't see it very well, but could follow enough of the picture to be able to keep up with what was going on. I was very glad, finally, to be able to use the present my colleagues from the bank had given me when I first became ill, a combined TV and video. This was a huge change, as the hours from now on would not weigh quite so heavily on me all the time. I would now be able to distract myself for short periods with TV, and that had to be better than staring holes into the ceiling.

Having gone through the whole business of trying out various wheelchairs in the previous hospital, I now found myself being put through the whole process again. Perversely, my transfer to this hospital did not include my wheelchair, so, while a brand new one was being planned, funded and manufactured by the hospital wheelchair department, I clearly had to have a temporary 'loan' chair for the interim. I ended up with something that reminded me of the discomfort of an economy-class seat on a long-haul flight. It felt a bit like being wedged between two seats in a row of three on a commuter train, with my knees pushed up so far that they were almost dangling from my ears, an all-too-familiar experience for me with my long legs. I had been a commuter for four years and had endured that sitting position on trains in and out of London on every working day during that time. Hunched in this temporary wheelchair, I sometimes felt like the eternal commuter, stuck for hours, even days like that, unable to escape. Just another nightmare scenario played out in my head.

As time went on, I was becoming more and more aware of how even the apparently most trivial of problems could conspire to make life difficult, even dangerous, for me. The pillows here, for example, seemed to pose a startling problem to me at night. They appeared to be very fond of my face, so much so that, as my body slipped slowly down the bed during the night hours, they had a tendency to wrap themselves around it, and sometimes even to cover it completely. It was not uncommon for the night staff to come in in the morning and have to rescue me from underneath a pillow. Five minutes like that is bad enough, but several hours spent in semi-suffocation is definitely not funny.

A feeling similar to pins and needles, which always tended to plague those areas particularly affected by the stroke, especially the whole of my left side, became a daily irritation. Sometimes this sensation could last in excess of two hours, and could be set off by something as slight as a single touch to one area. I thought I would never be free of it, but about four months after the stroke, it began to subside and finally it disappeared. No one ever knew about it.

On the more positive side, one serious improvement in my care soon made life a little easier. This was the demarcation line drawn when the very uncomfortable suction procedure was finally left behind. The rehab staff here decided to withdraw it and, very early on, began to help me to manage without it. The weaning off process took about a fortnight, and, after this extended cold turkey, I never looked back.

Another positive thing was the fact that, in spite of my trachi, it was not considered necessary for us to be accompanied at all times. Catherine and I checked out the surroundings whenever we could, taking the wheelchair through the gardens, sitting on the terrace on fine days, or with Catherine reading to me in the beautiful library, which had a lovely Wedgwood-like stucco ceiling.

This hospital, with its ward and staff dedicated to rehabilitation, had specially built shower rooms with enough shower trolleys to give us a shower three times a week and a proper wash on other days. This represented a significant improvement for me, although it was something so basic to my life before the stroke that in those days I had never thought anything of it. Now, however it had become vital.

Daily Reminders

This is a place where no-one can ignore reality, where life presents itself as a vision of all that is monstrous, unfair and inhuman. Severe brain injury is random in its choice of victim and every patient here has been profoundly affected. Each day Hasso is confronted by one proof after another of what it means to suffer this condition, and his frailty is mirrored in the fate of others.

At first he was too ill to leave the ward, but as soon as he was well enough to face longer periods in his wheelchair, I was allowed to wheel him about unaccompanied. This was a novelty at first because previously we had been prevented from leaving the ward without a nurse. I was very nervous the first day in case he should start to choke or suddenly become unable to breathe.

But, little by little, we have built up the time spent off the ward, until I am now able to take him away for longer and longer periods at a time. Pushing him through the corridors and into the elegant public rooms has brought a new sense of limited but precious freedom. We try to find quiet places each day in either the library, the ballroom or on the terrace, where, needless to say, we also encounter many other residents, alone, propelling themselves along in their electric wheelchairs, or sometimes accompanied by visiting family members.

I have never lost my urge to protect Hasso from the sights

and sounds of those who share this place with him. It seems irrational, but I hate the feeling that he is exposed each day to reminders of where he is and why; even though, inevitably, those reminders come in the shape of his fellow patients. It is therefore not without some degree of trepidation that I wheel him through the hospital grounds and busy areas in search of a quiet corner.

But this is also a place of contradictions and often of goodness, because here, in the midst of such terrible suffering, there is sometimes real kindness. So many of the staff are warm and supportive. Each day I see small acts of genuine empathy and compassion. The reality of this kindness has affected Hasso in a subtle way. Weary as he is, he seems a little calmer.

The nurses here try to be gentle and the care assistants are mostly kind. They make an effort to see him as a person, still whole and intact. They have seen a few cases like his. Since this is a national centre for extreme brain injury it is one of the very few places that have.

There is even one other patient here who has experienced the same kind of stroke. That's extremely rare. Not that she and Hasso can communicate with each other. But he is attentive to all that is said around him and I know he has heard about her. He becomes sharply aware when the nurses talk about her or when they pass each other in their respective wheelchairs in the corridors. I sense a strange ineffable bond between them that I find hard to understand, but which is very real. Sometimes he asks me about her. She is a mother with young children. Their rooms are next to each other and when I leave at night I see her lying there in the semi-darkness, immobile like Hasso and alone. I can't begin to bear what my imagination tells me she feels. Sometimes in my mind as I travel home I see them both lying in their parallel rooms. It's eerie and unreal. A kind of curious kinship.

A Blackbird's Lament

Moving from the first hospital meant a number of improvements for me, it is true, but I was still in London, only a stone's throw away from the location of the big grand slam at Wimbledon and within earshot of trains, traffic and the general pandemonium of the city. For someone who loves country life, this new location was more bearable, but still a long way from the sights and sounds I need to be near. I love listening to the sad lament of the blackbird, the occasional fluting of the great woodpecker and the hissing bark of a fox. At home, I had often sat out in my garden late into the night to hear the hooting of the tawny owl. Usually at around midnight on a warm summer's night, when the whole family were in bed, I liked to wander into the garden in the dark, when the air was still and calm. I would often find myself under the big apple tree at the back of the garden, listening to all the sounds on the night air. I also used to lie awake in the early hours looking forward to the short but intense burst of the dawn chorus, the constant chattering of the wild geese passing overhead and the far distant moan of a cow somewhere in the damp meadow, complaining about the morning dew.

In place of these comforting country sounds, I would now lie in my bed listening to the wailing sirens of the three emergency services, the almost rhythmic rattling of a train deep down in the valley accompanied by a sort of repetitive thud (probably caused by trains passing over the same sleeper), the slowing down of the cars at the nearby traffic lights, the voices of the staff on night duty, the TVs blaring out in other rooms, and the laughter of people outside my door.

Part of the pain of being imprisoned in hospital for so long is that you have to suffer the immense sadness of being interminably separated from all that you love ... your family, friends, loved ones, and your own environment, plus your own space, your privacy, as well as the sense of well-being that feeds the soul and gives life a purpose and meaning. I missed all of these so intensely that it was almost as hard to bear as my bodily imprisonment.

'A One-Off'

It's odd that there are things I never knew about Hasso. I'm coming to see that there are plenty of them. When friends and colleagues visit him from work, some of whom I have never met before, I see a different side to him. I have to remind myself, I suppose, that it was an illusion to think I knew all about him. Although we have been married for seventeen years, he has spent much of his daily life in the company of others at work and I have only rarely caught a glimpse of that part of his life.

When his work colleagues and friends visit the hospital, they like to fill him in on gossip and to reminisce. Once they have adjusted to their initial horror of seeing him like this and manage to adopt an artificial but reassuring 'naturalness' with him, they generally manage to communicate their very genuine affection and this brings him a lot of pleasure. I think that they feel a deep sense of satisfaction if they can amuse him or prompt him, by means of spelling out the words with his eyes via me, to converse with them. It must feel to them a kind of defiance of the new rules that bind him in this steel-tight brace of silence. Perhaps it is like a small, but not insignificant, triumph. I suspect that he knows this and that his participation is, in turn, a kind of gift to them. It moves him intensely, this loyalty, this refusing to accept that he has changed, this never giving up on him.

Recently, while talking to Hasso's boss, Peter, I learned something entirely new about him. Something he has never told me. It turns out that a short while before Hasso had his stroke they were visiting a banking convention in Germany together. One evening, they heard there was a special reception being held at a luxury lakeside hotel in the Bavarian Alps. It seemed like too good an opportunity to miss. In order to get close to the clients and do a bit of networking, they decided to attend. The trouble was that when they got there, they discovered that it was a very formal do and the delegates were being admitted by invitation only. The president of the Bavarian Banking Union was greeting everyone personally at the door. Hasso and Peter, of course, had no invitation. Peter told me that at this point he was ready to call it a day and beat a path back to their hotel, but before he could stop him, Hasso had gone straight up to the door, was shaking the president's hand and introducing them both to him. Before Peter knew what was happening, he was following Hasso across the floor of the restaurant to a table with two spare places, and within minutes they were seated next to the very people they had been keen to meet, chatting away as if they were old friends. According to Peter, it turned out to be a great evening and, as well as being so enjoyable, the contacts they made that night actually turned out to be good business for the bank.

Peter seemed surprised that I'd never heard the story. I looked over at Hasso. He was obviously enjoying this. Peter joked that this was 'vintage Hasso' and that he was well known for behaving as if he owned the place. He hastened to add that, rather than putting people's backs up, it was part of his easy-going charm and it was as unconscious as it was endearing. Peter had a real glint in his eye as he told me all this. Glancing sideways at Hasso as he spoke, he winked at me and said, 'This guy's a one-off'.

When Peter had left, the staff arrived for the evening drug round. I watched Hasso's face as the nurse gave him his medication through the tubes. He was staring at me and I could swear that there was more than a ghost of a smile in his eyes. I was still puzzling over the fact that I had never heard this story before. Clearly, he had been enjoying the moment, and most of all my reaction to it. He seemed to be relishing the fact that I hadn't known anything about it. It amused him to think that I was discovering aspects of him that I hadn't known before. As the nurse busied herself, he gazed steadily into my eyes, watching the smile spread across my face. The pleasure stirring in him was palpable. And so, it has to be said, was mine.

The Cold Shower

It was now over four months since I had had my stroke and, although I had clearly begun to emerge from the shadows that had been lurking around me and that had almost claimed me, I was obviously not, in any real sense, getting any better. Improvement, I was told, would be painfully slow, taking months, even years. At this point, it didn't seem to be happening at all. Indeed, after so much time, it didn't seem as if it was ever likely to. I was not about to give up hope entirely, but I was, to say the least, not best pleased with everything.

Left to its own devices, my mind was caught in a constant struggle between desperate optimism and blank pessimism. It was time to wash my head under cold water. My doctor had the courage to provide the cold water. She was very frank and I very much appreciated the serious talk we had, which was, I knew, long overdue. The situation was bleak. Life would have to be lived, if one could call it that, at a slow pace and on a completely different plane from now on. Acceptance was the key, she told me, and her words were unequivocal. She could hardly know, though, how devastating this was for me. The pain of this was unbearable.

How was I, who had always been so fiercely independent, to cope with this? How could the mischievous boy I had always carried within the man I had become, so addicted to freedom, ever accept being so totally entombed? How was I to bear it?

The deafening silence I received in answer to this question was testament to the pain I would have to face now and in the future.

My doctor was a woman of the greatest compassion and she became my one salvation in this place. Her honesty was a mark of her courage and from now on she fought the anguish in me with all the wit and humour she could muster. She was well acquainted with German culture and literature. Having given me the nickname 'Sir Knight', she would greet me with a flourish whenever our wheelchairs approached each other in the long corridors. I came to look forward to her twice-daily visits, and felt comforted by her kindness and devotion in the face of such terrible odds.

Rehabilitation, or such that was envisaged for me, meant a daily programme of therapy sessions, leaving the weekend free for us to fill as best we could. Most of my time was now spent trying to build up my stamina and preventing further deterioration. Hoisted into my wheelchair every morning, I was now no stranger to how it felt to sit motionless, like a wet blanket, all day, unable to shift my weight or respond to the need that was screaming out inside me to get up and run as far away as possible from my imprisonment.

The inability to change anything at all was a terrible new feeling, an alien thing, which clamped me down and against which my spirit never ceased to struggle. Acceptance was inconceivable. Rebellion, however, was a physical impossibility. But not in spirit. Through all the pain and the hurt, it was my spirit I felt strengthening itself in its resolve.

There were times, though, when the true nature of my helplessness was hard to swallow. About a year after this, for example, when I had been home for a few days, the point was driven home again with exquisite (though probably unwitting) cruelty, when one district nurse commented to another, in a nonchalant, matter-of-fact tone, that I was really unable to do anything at all. It hit the nail on the head, of course, but it felt as if I had been pushed into a black hole. The truth was that I couldn't even move my wheelchair from A to B on my own. I was now to be entirely dependent on the kindness of others. Inevitably, my frightful level of dependency meant that a lot of time would, from now on, be spent waiting for others to do things for me, while I busily attempted to stare holes in the air.

Even today, after so much time, everything I do, be it a thousand tiny, often invisible muscle movements a day, never has the desired result. The few muscles over which I have regained a little control (in my eyes, my right hand and my head) do not seem to follow any known rules. The lack of oxygen to the brain during the stroke has caused the total loss of access to any upward movement in the few muscles I have left, because I can press down a bit, but not up. The little that has returned, however, has regrown like the muscles of a newborn baby in the body of a grown-up.

This was especially noticeable with my tongue, which by now had advanced from public enemy number one to my arch enemy, because the weakness in its muscles meant that it constantly fell backwards inside my mouth and kept blocking my windpipe. In order to avoid choking on my own tongue, I had to try to drop my head forward. Sometimes I am simply not able to do this, and so end up coughing and spluttering with my tongue blocking off the air and making me gag. So, I found myself between a rock and a hard place – I basically had a choice between zero visibility with my head down and, literally, a pain in the neck, or choking with my head up, struggling to breathe.

This lack of control impacts on basic practical issues both large and small. Cleaning my teeth, for example, became a huge problem. In the previous hospital, Catherine used to brush them as quickly as possible and use a syringe to rinse my mouth out; then, before the water had a chance to slip down my throat and start choking me again, she quickly used a suction machine to suck it all out. At home now we have to manage as well as we can without such equipment. The whole operation is complicated by the fact that my teeth are always tightly clenched, something that I am unable to control, and, in addition, I am now extremely ticklish on the gums inside my teeth, which doesn't make things any easier. In fact, teeth cleaning is still a daily battle.

Strange sensations also began to accompany the parts of my body that twitched or involuntarily went into spasm. The raising of my upper lip, which happens without my bidding and feels as if I'm curling my lip (which must give an extremely unpleasant impression to onlookers), nearly always causes a tingling reaction which originates in the last joint of my thumb, and usually spreads to the first two fingers of my otherwise lifeless left hand. I imagine that both areas are either positioned in close proximity in the brain, or that they share the same pathway. Such odd phenomena made me speculate a lot about such things.

As a young boy, I had once read with horror about sudden loss of muscle power. Now, I had first-hand experience of it. The horror, incidentally, is undiminished. In a bizarre stroke of irony, I came across a strangely parallel example of my fate while languishing in the first hospital. Locked-in syndrome, rare as it is, is depicted with startling accuracy in the very first 'talking book' I was given in hospital: *The Last Jew*, by Noah Gordon. I can only presume that the kind relative who sent it to me was totally unaware of its contents. I could hardly believe my ears when I heard how a character in the novel is struck down with exactly the same kind of stroke as I had experienced. The description of inertia and the expressionless face, with the half-moon–shaped mouth pointing downwards, like mine, is uncannily accurate. What were the odds, I mused, of the very first story chosen for my distraction containing this sort of description? Life had become so bizarre by now that everything seemed to reflect and resound with reminders of my fate. Even in fiction, I was confronted with what I was trying to forget.

A Visit from Home

I always love watching Hasso and Wichard together. Hasso has always been very fond of all his siblings and has been so glad of their visits to the hospital. Of necessity his sisters' visits have had to be short, but I know how he has valued them. Somehow, though, the time Wichard spends with him, squeezed as it has to be into his own busy professional life back in Germany, is very special to Hasso. For me the love between them has always been intensely moving, perhaps because it is so infrequently expressed in words but has only gestures, humour and the bond of a shared past to express itself. These visits cost Wichard so much emotionally. He works very hard to cheer Hasso, to distract him with silly stories and to inspire him to greater courage and hope, but his voice often betrays his emotion and the tears are hard for him to restrain when he leaves the room on the pretext of a quick cigarette outside.

As Hasso's younger brother, Wichard has never known life without him. Although we have lived in different countries now for a very long time, the pull between them has never weakened. Different in appearance and nature as any two brothers can be, they nevertheless show the occasional trait of bewildering and uncanny similarity. They share, for example, a quirky skill for humorously bending and shaping their native language for comic effect, making them sound sometimes eerily alike. They both enjoy life's many pleasures and seem to agree that the pleasure is generally enhanced if experienced in each other's company. Two years ago, Wichard arranged with me to turn up to Hasso's fortieth birthday here in England unannounced. Hasso had absolutely no idea he was coming. Wichard and his wife, Heike, drove all the way with my brother who lives near them in Germany, arriving to catch Hasso completely by surprise. I'll never forget the look on his face when he opened the door. His joy was immense. They were both genuinely delighted to see each other and to be able to spend precious time together.

For Hasso, Wichard has always been an important part of himself and he has loved him and his two sisters with an intensity that has never failed to move me. The two brothers in particular lived their lives very much intertwined with each other before I came along. When I met Hasso, he was sharing a house with Wichard and they also shared holidays, friends and jokes. In the early days of our marriage, when I was adjusting to my new life in Germany, it was frequently Wichard who would keep me company when Hasso was at work. Being on shift work, he was often around during the day and we shared tea or went out to lunch. I have nice memories of those days and they make Wichard's sadness all the more poignant to me. I see his hands tremble as he enters Hasso's room and hear the crack in his voice as he leans down over the bed to kiss him. I can only guess at his feelings and at the depth of his grief.

When Wichard finally brought their parents all the way here to the hospital to visit, Hasso faced one of the most difficult days so far. In fact, the experience was so emotional he has not wanted to discuss it since that day. It was the first time since the stroke that they had been able to come and the last three months have wrought such terrible changes on their son. No amount of explaining and support can prepare a parent for such a moment. His mother seemed to have come to the end of something. Quiet and bemused before the immensity of what has befallen her child, she struggled to find a way to react, coming face to face with the realisation that for this there is no formula to fall back on, no roadmap, no script. The stern courage that Hasso's father has applied to all the adversity in his own life was not enough to help him through that day. Now in a wheelchair himself after years of struggling with disability since his early twenties, his own sufferings seemed to pale at the sight of his once robust and handsome elder son. The effect on both Hasso's father and mother was as crushing and heart-breaking as I had feared.

The day was warm and, to help dispel some of the grief and shock which had been so palpable during the first moments of their meeting, I suggested we try to get Hasso up into the wheelchair so that he could spend some time with them in the fresh air of the hospital grounds. But outside, while we waited for the staff to get him ready, I tried to explain that Hasso's condition had deteriorated so much that he might not be able to endure more than half an hour in the wheelchair. I had tried several times before then to explain the seriousness of Hasso's condition, to warn them that he was hovering very near the edge and that his resilience was being sorely tested, but it took that first half-hour of shock and horror to make them fully understand.

Hasso himself was finding all this even harder than they were. Though he had long wished for them to be there, he had also been dreading this. He knew only too well that it is the kind of shock that a parent will never recover from and that the agony of seeing one's own child suffer is often more acute than one's own pain. He also knew that it would cut him up to see their reaction.

To make matters worse, they had arrived on one of the hardest days in the past few weeks. His temperature had remained sky-high over recent days, the frequent vomiting was still not under control and he was so dreadfully weak. The effort to endure that day cost him dearly. Unaccustomed as they were to the absence of facial expression in him and to his inability to speak, his parents struggled to fill the long silences. It fell largely to Wichard to help. As I walked away from them on the terrace to allow them some time alone, I couldn't help the surge of sadness that engulfed me as I turned and glanced at that sad little group in the sunshine. Before long Wichard had come to find me. Hasso wanted to go in; he couldn't take any more.

In truth it was one of the saddest days. Hasso's parents left later that afternoon along with Wichard on the long, arduous journey home. Hasso sank back into himself and avoided my eyes for the rest of the day. Between bouts of vomiting and the struggle to breathe through the secretions blocking his trachi, he stared straight ahead of him with a kind of detached wistfulness.

Far away, down through the corridors of memory, he seemed to be drifting out of reach. I didn't try to haul him back. Somewhere, it seemed to me, through the sunlit long grass in the fields of his childhood, he was seeking some memory, some image to hold on to. Some moment when the three faces round his bed that day had held joy and laughter rather than the horror and shock he had not failed to see. It was an image I could not give him. But as a great sigh lifted his chest and slowly petered out, I hoped with all my heart that he would find it somewhere.

The Mountain Comes to Mohammed

Ill as I was, during the late summer after my parents' visit, I was about to have another deeply moving experience. My long-lost friend from secondary-school days, whose memory had come to me so often when I lay there, waiting and waiting, during my first few months in hospital, had lost touch with me over the years. We had first met at school and did many things together until we both joined up for our military service. His grandmother taught me all about mushrooms and from his father I learned how to keep rabbits. We were inseparable and lived in a world centred on catching field mice and sticklebacks and making our own bows and arrows. Though I hadn't seen him for so long, he remained in my memory as a gentle person, with blond shoulder-length hair and laughing eyes and a moustache. Though I had often thought of him, we hadn't seen each other for many years. He had never even met Catherine. We had been friends, literally, from the very first day of secondary school, and, for me, he always embodied my memories of happy carefree childhood days. Quite by chance, he had recently met my brother who told him what had happened to me. He wrote to me and then, within a few weeks, flew over for the day to visit me. I think it was very emotional for him, as it was for me, and he spent a lot of the time just sitting with me, holding my hand, remembering. A few weeks later, he returned with my brother, determined to cheer me up. They sat by my bed for hours, telling wickedly funny stories and jokes and we laughed as if there would be no tomorrow. Catherine left us alone together until they had to go, which was a particularly sad moment. It was, however, a day I will never forget. The day the mountain came to Mohammed.

Following on a rather damp summer came a very wet autumn and widespread flooding was the result. It was good to be up on high ground, as it began to feel like the great flood in the book of Genesis. One downpour followed another and threatening clouds seemed to be a permanent fixture on the weather map, particularly in the south-east of England.

Coincidentally, Catherine was reading Jules Verne's *Twenty Thousand Leagues Under the Sea* to me during the day. I used to imagine her travelling back and forth to the hospital through torrential downpours and rivers of water, in something more resembling the *Nautilus* than a car. She refused to let the atrocious weather keep her from coming to the hospital every day, even though it now took her hours longer to complete the journey as huge detours were necessary to avoid the flooded areas. Sometimes she was forced to stay overnight in the cottage set aside for visitors in the hospital grounds, but this was not ideal, as it kept her from seeing the children for that tiny part of the day still reserved for them in the evening and early morning. Low-lying tunnels and underpasses filled up with water and the journey became like 'Mission Impossible', on one occasion taking all of three hours one way. Public transport was not really an alternative because 'the wrong kind of rain' was repeatedly responsible for cancelled buses and trains. The storms lasted for weeks and transformed the countryside into lakes. The children were sent home from school as the waters rose. Rain battered on my windowpanes at night, and I lay awake imagining how the family at home would be coping.

As Christmas approached, a long overdue renovation project for the ward I was on was started, including the installation of a new alarm system for patients and some redecorating. For us, this meant that we would have to vacate the ward entirely to make room for the painters. We were moved up to the top floor on the other side of the hospital and would stay there for over six weeks. An L-shaped single room became my new home and it had the benefit of a good view over the surroundings. Finally, my OTs had also come up with a way of operating the alarm–call system (which I had never been able to use, even when I desperately needed help) by way of my hand splint, using a single switch and operated with a small adaptor. Now, as long as my hand did not slip off the splint, which unfortunately often happened, I could finally summon help during the night. This was an important step.

In this hospital, my trachi was changed monthly using a special kind of gel and this was carried out very quickly. That swift action, when performed skilfully, was more bearable than my other experiences had been, especially when the nurse used a lubricant. As I was there so long, I had ample chances to experience this and to judge the relative skills of those performing the job. Breathing, however, was actually becoming more and more of a problem as time went on. The stroke had literally swept away so many of my essential elements. Breathing, mere breathing, something so basic, so second nature, had become a real struggle.

My doctor now decided, however, that it was time to see if I could live without the trachi tube altogether. It was essential to know whether I could be helped to begin breath-ing normally again through my mouth and not through this hole in my throat. The tube was now blocked off regularly every day for ever-increasing lengths of time. She now took to calling me 'der rote Ritter' (the Red Knight), as the colour of the cap used to block off the tube was bright red. In time, she became very amused by the new name she had devised for me: 'Rotkäpchen' (Red Riding Hood), a play on words, of course, as the direct translation is 'little red cap'.

The experience was terrible at first, as it felt like suffocating or drowning and was not only very hard work, but also extremely distressing. I dreaded it, but knew it would be better if it meant that, in the end, I could manage to live more normally. The worst stage came when I had to go all night with the 'plug' in, gasping and wheezing, unable to control my breathing in any way at all, just hoping that in time things would improve. One night, however, I had one of my usual coughing fits. This was nothing out of the ordinary, and I often felt as if these fits were choking me. Well, this one was really something else. It must have worried the nurse on duty, who eventually came to my room to check on me. She took one look at me and rapidly disappeared to fetch something. I knew something was wrong, but I couldn't actually see what it was. I didn't realise that my coughing fit had been so violent that I had actually coughed out the whole of the trachi tube in my throat. I was lying there with a hole in my neck and didn't even realise what had happened. I had managed to get rid of it without the necessary medical attention. The nurse came rushing back with a replacement.

Very soon, however, it was decided that, in light of what had happened that night, I should be made to spend more and more time trying to breathe without the trachi. Very slowly, things did improve slightly and eventually it was removed completely. I have now been without the trachi for over two years. Breathing has never been easy, nothing like it was before, but I did win a victory over the tyranny of the trachi and this, more than anything, made it possible, finally, for me to leave hospital behind me and come home.

However, this event brought with it another crushing disappointment. I had hoped, somewhat naïvely perhaps, that somehow, with the removal of the trachi, my voice might begin to return. I knew that this was hoping for a lot, but I couldn't bear the thought that I would never be able to speak again, so hope stubbornly, though perhaps unrealistically, continued to burn within me. To my deep disappointment, my voice has never returned. So I am condemned to silence, and to relying upon Catherine's uncanny ability to read my thoughts, as well as the messages I spell out with my eyes. Since that time, many people have taken the trouble to learn the spelling method, so it is sometimes possible for me to join in conversations, albeit in a very long-winded way. Now, with hindsight, I know that such optimism was very naïve. The disappointment, though, was shattering. My ability to communicate spontaneously with those around me and the familiar sound of my own voice had quite simply abandoned me, never to return.

Meanwhile, life had become peppered with all the minor misunderstandings and irritations that result from the lack of effective communication. The loss of the speed and efficiency of just being able to say the words I needed was incredibly frustrating. Sentences have the habit of being a bit like scorpions – always watch out for the sting in the tail. If a sentence is cut short, it's quite possible the meaning will be completely misunderstood. Such misunderstandings often caused consternation and for me frequent disappointment. Unable as I was to correct the muddles, they were often never cleared up, and there was nothing I could do about it. Sometimes a single word would have sufficed to put things right, but, of course, this was beyond me.

The tedium of this life was something to be endured, as we had little or no means of altering the day-to-day structure of the routine, or total arid lack of it, at weekends. One way of conquering the utter desert of time at weekends emerged when Catherine discovered she would be able to borrow an ambulance for a few hours and take me out. Once she had completed a day's instruction, she was able to collect the keys and the prison doors were flung open. I had visions of us tasting the freedom of escape in the spirit of Mr Toad in his new motorcar, 'the only way to travel'.

Actually, inevitably for us, it wasn't quite as simple as that: a qualified nurse had to come with us each time and this had to be arranged well in advance; Catherine had to learn to manhandle the wheelchair into position in the ambulance and secure it safely with ratchets and bolts on the floor (a job normally done by two ambulance men) and we had to choose some kind of suitable destination for our 'family outing', while all the time pretending that this was something approaching normality. We made a few trips to a local market and to Richmond Park, but it was winter and I had been inside hospital walls since May and could only endure short bursts outside, where the temperature felt to me more like Alaska than West London. However, those little trips on bleak and dreary Sundays, accompanied by my family, were a sad but real attempt at being a family again. I will never forget the wonderful feeling of togetherness it gave me.

A Normal Sunday

'Why don't you come over to this side of the table so you can be closer to your feet?'

It's the kind of question the children are used to hearing. He delivers it with his usual irony and Christian guffaws, spraying and dribbling cornflakes and milk as he does so. Hasso wipes his sleeve in an exaggerated fashion, glancing at me with a glint in his eye and feigning disgust at his son's unaristocratic behaviour. Lucia groans and removes her feet from the chair next to him.

'Pappi ...' Christian begins, the cornflakes only half chewed. But before he can take a breath to continue, Hasso stops him with the pseudo-military command to keep his mouth shut while eating. He avoids my eyes across the table, making an effort to remain serious. Sophia and Lucia have both noticed the intended edge in his tone. He isn't angry. He speaks German to the children, as he usually does, and as always his voice is gentle and mischievous. It is more coaxing than harsh and contains more studied disappointment than reproach. Though intended as a reprimand, it is a stone tossed into the water which hardly even makes a ripple. The children are accustomed to this kind of insistence. Though he likes at times to create the impression of being a disciplinarian, it never really works. They are no more afraid of him than they are in awe. But table manners, as everyone knows, are their father's minor obsession.

Christian hurriedly chews and swallows and tries again.

'Pappi . . .'

'Yes . . .'

'Well, I told Jake at school the other day that Apa once ate a worm for a bet, but he didn't believe me.'

A pause while Hasso takes an inordinately long time to finish his mouthful of toast before resuming. The girls exchange amused raised eyebrows. I join in. I know what's coming.

'That's probably because he has never met your grandfather.'

'Yes, but is it true, did he really eat a worm? A whole worm?'

Hasso turns to him in mock surprise. 'Of course he did. Don't you believe it?'

'YUK! Yuk, yuk, yuk! A whole worm!' He's twisting and gyrating his little body on the chair next to Hasso, imitating the worm's slow descent down his grandfather's throat. 'That's disgusting!'

'Yes, it is,' Hasso replies, enjoying Christian's reaction. 'It really is *disgusting*.' He lays special emphasis on the word, making snake-like gestures with his flattened hands which cause squeals and more wriggling from Christian. He's really warming to his subject now. The girls are enjoying this. 'But it was also an extremely wise business decision and showed he wasn't slow to recognise a financial opportunity when it came along.'

The words wash over Christian and leave him behind. He's playing with his spoon in the soggy cereal, stirring the limp flakes around in a circle. He's still thinking of the worm. Slowly the vague meaning of the words catch up with him.

'But why did he really do it?'

'For money, of course.'

Christian's brow furrows. He screws up his eyes. 'How much?'

'One mark.'

'Is that a lot?'

'Not really, but it was a lot to him, he was about your age and it was worth about . . .'

'Go on, Pappi,' says Sophia, 'I bet you're going to tell us exactly, down to the last penny!'

Hasso frowns in mock concentration, his lips silently moving in calculation of the exchange rate of the old German mark circa 1930. He's only half joking. I can't restrain a smile.

'Oh no!' laughs Lucia. 'This is going to be just like the sausages around the world!'

'What?' Christian is lost.

'At the village party? . . . When Pappi won the quiz? . . . Because he was the only person in the room who knew how many sausages it would take to go round the world!'

'Oh yes, I remember! How did you do it, Pappi?' He's forgotten the worm.

'Well, that one was easy. Let's say the average sausage is about 10 cm long,' he gestures the length of a sausage with a finger and thumb. 'It's a small sausage . . .' he concedes, cocking his head slightly to the side. They all nod. '. . . and the circumference of the earth is more or less 40,000 kilometres . . .' He looks at me for approval, but can see from the blank look on my face that I haven't got a clue. 'So,' he continues with a smile, 'it's just a question of moving the decimal point a few times! 40,000 kilometres, 10 sausages per metre, so that makes . . . 400 million sausages!'

'Wow! They'd need a lot of ketchup for all those sausages!'

'God, no!' I say as he looks round for a pen, guessing that he's already started calculating the number of ketchup bottles required.

'OK,' he laughs, 'but converting the old German mark to today's money is a bit harder than the sausages . . .'

The girls are reminiscing about the sausage incident. I remember the look of amused satisfaction that had crossed his face at the time when the entire village hall was agonising over their intricate conversions of sausages to inches, feet, furlongs and miles. He quickly scribbled the answer to the quiz team captain who startled the whole hall with his calculation which came to within a few hundred sausages. There was thunderous applause. It had been their first taste of him, just after we moved to the village, and for once he'd actually enjoyed all the banter about Germans and 'Vorsprung' and precision because he knew that the first evening had endeared him to them.

He resumes his calculations, reaching for a pen and, with a sidelong wink at me, scribbles figures down the side of the front page of the newspaper. He's factoring in inflation and the cost of living and a large dose of baloney. Christian's face is rapt. The girls have started to chat about Boyzone.

With a grand flourish he circles the final figure and drops the paper into the centre of the table.

'A pound! It comes to about a pound.'

Christian's face drops. 'A pound? Is that all? Only a pound? He swallowed a worm for a pound?'

'Well it was a pound more than he had at the beginning of the day so it was worth it. It made sound financial sense, even if he was only about seven.'

'Yuk!' again. 'I wouldn't do it for a pound. I wouldn't do it for a measly pound. You'd have to pay me a lot more than that . . . at least . . .' he thinks desperately, 'at least . . . two pounds!'

Everyone laughs.

'I wouldn't do it for a hundred pounds!' says Lucia.

'I might do it for a hundred pounds,' ventures Sophia, and Hasso laughs so much that he almost sprays them all with tea.

'Pappi!' they all chorus in disgust.

A normal Sunday morning.

Dreaming of Home

It was now November and I began to get wind of talk that at first seemed unbelievable. Catherine was trying to negotiate with the hospital staff to get me home for a week or so at Christmas. In preparation for this, it was agreed that I could come home for a weekend visit. My occupational therapist agreed a date and time with Catherine to visit our home to see if the wheelchair would fit into the downstairs rooms. I realised that any access to the upstairs area, including our own bedroom, was out of the question, even long-term, because the house is far too small to have a lift fitted and there was no way I could ever use a stair-lift, as I can't sit unsupported. With a bit of rebuilding, it was decided that the lower floor would be just about accessible, though we would need a temporary ramp to access the house until anything more suitable could be built. At least this meant, to my relief, that we would not have to move altogether; but we would have to organise quite a dramatic rethink of the layout of the ground floor.

In preparation for the planned Christmas leave, the district nurses got their heads together with several hospital people, and I was given the chance to try out life alone with my family for a weekend in the hospital flat. This consisted of a few rooms put aside by the rehab team for patients going through the transitional stages of discharge after long hospitalisation, and was designed to help families towards independent living, with the close proximity of nursing staff on hand to help if the need arose. Catherine and the children stayed there with me over the weekend, managing all on our own for the first time. This was quite a success, although the whole thing was a very strange experience. The odd thing was that the flat was located in a part of the hospital that was entirely deserted at the weekends: a strange, rather cold environment, which we all found very eerie, especially the children. Still, it persuaded the powers that be that we were capable of living independently without hospital staff and, in that respect, was a significant step towards coming home.

The next big change came with a move back to my old ward, but this time in a shared room. I found this very difficult, but, fortunately it was not to be for too long, as, after a week or so, the long-awaited Christmas break actually arrived.

Everybody could feel the festive season approaching, and even I began to feel something of the Christmas spirit building up. I could hardly believe the feelings rushing through me as I found myself homeward-bound, belted up securely in the back of a steadily moving ambulance. The first time in eight months. This break-out had involved weeks of planning, organisation and no end of persuasion to make it happen. As I travelled away from London with Catherine sitting next to me in the back of the ambulance, I recognised some of the various back roads. I noticed the urban clearways with their double red lines, then the more familiar territory of the London Orbital, the famous M25. From now on, the more recognisable landmarks helped me to monitor the progress of the vehicle. I had driven this road so many times and had never imagined I would travel down it like this. Moving round it anticlockwise, I recognised the junction to Gatwick which I had so often used.

Then came the service station where I remembered having

filled up the removal lorry containing all our belongings, which I had driven to Kent from Devon just a few years before. Having been trained in the army to drive all manner of lorries, I had not felt that anxious about driving an HGV all that way. I had even driven an original American rocket launcher which had been battle-hardened in Korea and could be used for nuclear or conventional warheads. However, as I sat at the wheel of the removal van that day, I was reminded of how long it had been since I had been let loose on such a vehicle.

The Kent border sign flew past and then it was soon time to leave the M25, which in my experience had so often lived up to its reputation as the largest car park in Europe. I watched out of the ambulance window as we went up the dual carriageway towards my favourite spot, the top of the hill above our valley from where you have uninterrupted, far-reaching views over the countryside below. So often, when returning from business trips or from journeys to Devon, I had looked out for the tall conifers that mark the spot of our village in the valley below.

The view was only surpassed at sunrise, an experience which I loved and which I often saw in the mornings when returning from business in the US. A huge contrast, in the summer especially, to the Big Apple and the city that never sleeps. As the ambulance descended into the valley, my thoughts turned back to the hectic visits I had often made to New York, where I had had to get my head round a whole new kind of English, where a traffic jam was a back-up, a work permit a green card, and a turnpike a toll road. All familiar words, but with a different meaning over there. I had already got used to most of these in the way all Europeans do, and especially the British, namely through the TV, which gives you the uncanny feeling that you actually know a city like New York even before you have actually been there. So even the streets of New York, and all my memories of how it had felt to be working there, came flooding back as we neared home.

Moving steadily along the M25 in the direction of home, such thoughts served to knit together the glory days of my misspent youth, the optimistic happiness of family life and the now uncertain and bleak present which was mine.

It was nearly Christmas, and, at this time of year, what little sun there was had already sunk low in the sky. Only the huge firs towered above the all-engulfing mist, with the exception of the odd plume of smoke rising up from nowhere, as everything seemed to be covered by the drifting fog. All was dipped first red, then yellow on top, leaving a white veil underneath. The combination of the elevated position and the ridge around the valley probably make it like a naturally walled garden, keeping in the ascending moisture from the reservoirs, ponds and the river, the dividing line between the so-called man of Kent and Kentish man, but also the traditional divide between the fruit and the hops.

Not far from our house, across the fields, is Penshurst Place, once owned by the Sidney family, whose name always made me think of Sydney, Australia. Australia was actually some-where I had always wanted to visit, but I had never managed to get there. I had often dreamed of the mysterious Ayres Rock and spotting dingoes in the Outback. Strange, how an English country house could make me think of that, simply through word association.

Winston Churchill was so enchanted by the position of a house not far from here that he bought it for the view and turned it into his beloved Chartwell. As my eye took in the gentle touch of the familiar, my thoughts wandered again to a lovely summer's day when we had visited Chartwell with Catherine's parents. I had been fascinated by one of the areas in the permanent exhibition of Churchill's times which contained photographs and newspaper reports about the sinking of the *Titanic*. I remembered my grandmother telling me that she had read about this in the newspaper, when still a very young girl at her home in Bärsdorf, Silesia. It has always amazed me how we are all somehow linked to the past and to each other by such tenuous threads, and by the memories of the eyewitness handed down to us in old age.

There had been so much happiness in my life in this place. With my thoughts wandering so far afield, it was difficult to reconnect with sober reality as the ambulance gathered speed downhill. There, on the left, for example, I noticed a lay-by where I used to stop to buy flowers for Catherine when returning home from my trips away. Soon afterwards came my exit, followed by the commuter station I used to use every day to make the journey up to the City. This was the last stretch, and one I knew so well. I had cycled along it every day, to and from the station. But that, of course, was in that far distant past when I had been someone else altogether.

I was indeed very emotional by this time, but was entirely unprepared for the effect that the first sight of the bend in the road and that small white ten-metre fence would have on me. Suddenly I felt a lump in my throat, and big tears began to roll down my cheeks. I wept as I had hardly done since I had left the house so many months before. Now I knew, finally, how much it all meant to me.

Balloons and banners festooned the hallway and the whole family was there to greet me. Unable to control my voice or my tears, I felt all my emotions come together. This was not how I had dreamt of coming home.

Ridiculously, there was also a very real mountain in the shape of my own front door to be negotiated. Two parallel, slippery metal ramps had been provided on temporary loan by local occupational therapists to get me up and over the two steps of my threshold. Funnily enough, I had never before taken much notice of those steps, and now they seemed to pose an almost insuperable barrier. Halfway up, with the wheelchair tilted at an alarming angle, the ramps began to bend rather worryingly in the middle. The whole weight of the chair combined with all of my weight was thrust back onto the limited strength of Catherine's arms, as she struggled to get me into the house safely. Fortunately, we were rescued by the male manpower of the two ambulance drivers who had accompanied us, and they were finally able to manoeuvre me successfully up the seemingly insurmountable makeshift entrance, with Catherine then shifting position and giving a helping hand from the front. I finally rolled into the house, home and dry at last, but in a manner resembling the arrival of a 'Push-me–pull-you', at the end of an emotionally charged, sentimental journey. We both realised, however, that this was definitely the best demonstration of how not to do it in future. A lot of changes would have to be made, just in order to get me in and out of the house, and, for the time being, I would be going absolutely nowhere.

Away from the hospital environment, for the first time in what felt like a lifetime, I began to reflect on my position from a different angle.

The doctors had told Catherine that relatively few people survive this kind of stroke and that survival, as such, had only been possible in recent years due to medical advances. I tried to force myself to contemplate the possible extent of the damage that had occurred in my own brain. This required pretty strenuous effort, as the newness of being at home in such a different state to the one I had been in while still well was a constant source of shock and horror. I tried at this stage, however, to comfort myself with the remarks made by my cousin, a doctor who has a practice in Hamburg. On the first of his many visits to me, quite early on, he had reminded me that it usually takes around three weeks for a little scratch alone to heal – and this job was obviously of quite a different order. So I had guessed back then that this could mean being 'off the air' for a considerable length of time, and that there were certainly no guarantees whatsoever of any recovery. I could see nothing but an uphill struggle ahead. But without the prospect of real recovery I found myself deeply troubled by a terrible sense of foreboding. It felt as if I had been forced to venture out into uncharted territory, but with the famous explorer spirit somewhat lacking.

While I worried about the long-term future, we muddled along as best as we could. Nevertheless, coming home, joyful though it was, was also a shock. Being looked after at home in a house where, as yet, no alterations had been carried out, was not ideal and it wasn't long before serious problems arose. These at least gave us food for thought and focused our plans on prioritising the improvements that would have to be made immediately. The hospital-type bed that had been found for me by the local health authority, for example, was far too short and had no electric controls. Only someone with experience of paralysed patients can possibly imagine how seriously difficult this made life. If you can't move at all, you can't shift your own weight in bed, and you definitely can't change position or hoist yourself up the bed as you slip down it. This has to be done by two people, one on either side of the bed, who roll and turn you in order to stretch out a sliding sheet underneath you, so you can then be pulled back up into position. In time, Catherine had to learn to move my entire weight around on her own, and to reposition me in bed at night without the help of a second pair of hands. The major problem that Christmas was that, even when positioned right up at the top, I was simply too long for the bed. It was decided that, in order to stop me slipping right down at night and ending up with my legs hanging down over the end of the bed towards the floor, it would be sensible to line the bed up to face the wall. Well, being paralysed is hardly the most stimulating kind of life in the first place, but having the scenic, uninterrupted panorama of a perfectly blank whitewashed wall to stare at most of the time was hardly conducive to mental stimulation. To make matters worse, the mattress I had been sent was little more than a rippled overlay, so thin and hard that it became horribly uncomfortable within less than half an hour. Lumps and bumps pressed into my body and the hardness began to cause pressure sores. Given that I was returned to bed at around 7 p.m., and had to stay there until about 10.30 a.m. the next day, this was not easy to endure.

Added to all that, ten days without a proper shower was no joke. I felt dirty and I had always hated being unwashed. For the moment, though, there was nothing better than bed baths on offer, so I had no alternative but to grin and bear it.

Catherine's plans for a shower room and a better arrangement for my bed would now go to the top of the agenda. Finding herself alone with the whole problem and, in the face of such lack of assistance from the usual public channels, she realised that she would simply have to get on with the project on her own and hope that, when it came to the actual alterations, friends and relatives could be galvanised into rolling up their sleeves and helping us out. To their credit, and it is something for which I shall always be grateful, this was actually what happened. In fact, the initial alterations to the house were to prove only the beginning of a magnificent response from many amazing people. Their efforts would make it possible, finally, to get me home and they would move heaven and earth to get the place into shape for a patient with my needs. And the transformation, when it came, was nothing short of miraculous.

For the time being, however, I spent the whole ten days of Christmas 'leave' at home in a state of pain and depression.

I have to admit that this often made me grumpy and even tearful. Frankly, it began to feel like the end of the world. I had been looking forward for so long to coming home and, no matter how hard everyone tried, I couldn't help feeling distraught. No one was to blame, but clearly a lot would have to change if I was to be able to live at home in future. In addition, I began to realise that the many months away from my children had made me rather intolerant of noise and the simple ups and downs of family life. Everything I had so missed and so looked forward to was now of very little comfort at all. I was unable to get over the huge sense of disappointment and this made me even more depressed.

In the face of this, Catherine and the children, in a desperate attempt to lift my spirits just a little, did their best to create something of the atmosphere of Christmas. The unmistakable, fresh aroma of pine sap from the Christmas tree in my room, together with the scent of real candles burning on its branches, was inevitably a powerful tug on the emotions. When we were finally alone in the evenings, they all sat on the edge of my bed, as the room glowed in the flickering light of the open fire and the candles. The children even managed the whole present-giving thing with as much enthusiasm and excitement as they could muster, drowning me in a pile of torn-off wrapping paper, and trying to keep the aromas of Christmas cooking and baking firmly behind the kitchen door to avoid torturing me any more. When they had gone to bed, Catherine sat silently beside me, holding my hand and watching the glow of the fire. There was no need to speak our thoughts. The quiet tears said it all.

I did a lot of thinking during those days at home, as I tried to make sense of the future. Although I felt the haunting sense of disappointment in what I was experiencing about being home, I began to realise this had a lot to do with not being able to take part in family life as I wanted to. This, clearly, was no one's fault. I could see that Catherine and the children had their own suffering to deal with as well as mine.

On reflection, I knew that life at home would be incomparably better than staying in hospital or residential care. The best in terms of distraction the hospital had to offer was three to four sessions of therapy a day. Sometimes, to the enormous frustration of the patient, these sessions were even cancelled at the last minute, usually because a therapist wanted to use the time to write reports about you, reports that would most likely remain unread by anyone.

Apart from therapy sessions, the rest of the time in hospital (late afternoons and evenings, weekends and bank holidays) was unbearably empty. Tedium had rapidly become my closest and most abiding enemy. Curiously enough, the longer you live with the desert of ever-extending time, the more difficult it gets to bear it. The yawning caverns of dead time in hospital are invariably punctuated by sharp reminders of the life whose doors have been slammed in your face and of being shunted onto a sideline to wait, while life and the living of it pass you by. You are reminded of it every time a doctor, nurse or carer goes off shift with a cheery 'goodbye' or you hear a car door close in the car park and the engine engage. It's then that the walls around you close in and the sky just beyond your window seems very far away.

Deep down I knew that for me there could really be nothing worse than never escaping from that kind of prison. I knew that I was far better off at home and that all I wanted now was to be with Catherine and the children. In addition, time could never drag as much at home as it did all the time in hospital. Indeed, I knew that if I was ever going to feel a tiny bit less depressed, this would only happen at home. I realised that by going home I would, albeit in a very limited way, finally be taking some control over my life again, and that this was the only chance I had to effect any serious changes at this moment in time. Knowing all of these things didn't immediately alleviate the depression, though. So, when I contemplated embarking on life at home as a completely different person from the one who had left it the year before, I was unable to stop the tears.

Wheelie

I V E G O T T H E ... The string of letters emerge on my notepad. Watching his eye blinks, I transfer the letters to the page. It's getting on for eleven and I'm bleary-eyed with leaden tiredness. I make a first attempt to identify whole words and separate out the patterns. 'I've got the . . .?'

He opens his eyes wide to signify agreement and we continue.

I N S R U ...

I haven't slept for more nights than I care to remember and I'm finding it hard to concentrate. I desperately want to lie down. Each few words take a monumental effort on Hasso's part, opening and closing his eyes as I go through the rows and columns of the alphabet chart to signify assent. It's a long and tedious process and requires patience and clear-headedness. We've only got ten letters down but it's taken us almost as many minutes. I rub my eyes and try to concentrate. The shapes of the letters are beginning to acquire a life of their own and to float about on the page.

Everyone has gone to bed, the carers who helped me to get him ready for bed left ages ago and we are alone. He lies in an awkward, rather outdated hospital bed in what used to be our living room. His first period at home has not been the homecoming he has been dreaming of for endless months. I am grateful that we can have him here with us and that we can at least start to reconstruct a vestige of what it was to live like a family again. But eight months of hospital life and the appalling reality of his condition have not been without their scars. He is frequently tearful and frustrated and often in pain.

It has been a deep sorrow to me to see how coming home seems to have broken his heart even more profoundly. I should have anticipated the rawness of his feelings and been aware that the sight of all he once knew would not gladden him as much as sadden him beyond endurance. I feel his disappointment in every bitter passing moment. There are so many practical problems. The bed we have been provided with is woefully inadequate for his level of disability and as a result he is constantly uncomfortable, in pain even. The hoist used for lifting him is not up to the job and, apart from being extremely unpleasant for him, is also difficult for me and for the carers to use, as it is manually operated and Hasso is very heavy. Moreover, the nurses and care assistants organised by our surgery have never been confronted with disability on this scale and are struggling to cope. They depend on a lot of input from me and I find myself obliged to work alongside them, showing them what I've learned from the skilled hospital staff. Added to this, no provisions have been made for washing beyond simple bed baths. Days on end without a shower have inevitably started to get Hasso down.

All these problems have accumulated over his time at home and have demonstrated to me how very much more we have to do before he comes home for good. He is overwrought and the depression seems to engulf him like a heavy coat, behind which he shrinks, collar up, unable to disguise his despair. I am so very worn down by his despair. It seeps like a noxious cloud through the pores of my skin and I again feel the sensation of falling, sinking, drowning.

Tonight, however, maybe he has looked at me and seen the strain. Perhaps he can see in my face the tiredness that weathers me and the effects of the desolation I try to hide from him. He is trying to put aside his own discomfort and distress and to engage me in conversation. As I was moving around the bed he blinked his eyes rapidly, the sign that he wanted to spell out a message. He seems more animated than of late and keen to tell me something. Through the treacle-like fog of my weariness, I feel him trying to throw me a line, to haul me in before the waves cover me. He is trying to buoy me up. But there is no hiding my exhaustion. I just wish he would sleep a little tonight and then we could spell this out in the morning. But he is insistent. Being wide awake, he can't sleep anyway, so I acquiesce.

I N S R U ...

What could he mean? There's a kind of throbbing pain at the front of my head which is only tiredness, but I can feel myself getting tetchy. My eyes are dry and occasionally drift off focus. There's a crick in my neck. Although I know it irritates him, I try to guess. Has he got the 'R' and the 'U' the wrong way round, I wonder? Is he trying to spell out another word?

'Insurance?' I try. 'Is it "insurance"?'

He closes his eyes firmly to show I'm on the wrong track.

I wobble the pencil between two fingers of my right hand trying to suppress the desire to yawn. His eyes are earnest and I realise this might be important. The possibility that he is in pain and trying to tell me suddenly shakes me awake and concentrates my mind. The letters stare back at me from the crowded note page. I bend my brain in the effort to decipher. I realise I'm being stupid: the 'R' and the 'U' couldn't be the wrong way round, as he is spelling them out linearly, one letter after the other. But, then again, maybe he's tired too and he's got them muddled up. It happens sometimes and can lead to all sorts of misunderstandings, especially when he's really washed out.

Concentrate, I tell myself. Perhaps it's not one word, but two. Three even. Maybe the 'R' and the 'U' mean 'your', or at a push, 'you're'. But that couldn't make sense either. I know I'm barking up the wrong tree. It's important to work this out in case some itch, or pain, or discomfort is driving him mad and I haven't noticed. I ask him, trying out various possibilities.

'You've got … a pain somewhere …?' I offer lamely. 'You've got something in my …' my voice peters out, the jumble of words raising only closed eyes and a slight shake of the head. The shake of the head is more a kind of tilting from side to side, a new development for Hasso and sometimes barely perceptible, which comes and goes with no obvious rhyme or reason.

None of the letters make sense. I'm not trying hard enough. I blink and adjust my position on the hard kitchen chair I have drawn up next to him. He tries again, his face betraying none of the impatience he must feel with me.

D O N T T R Y T O G U E S S (Don't try to guess.)

'OK, OK, I'm sorry,' I apologise.

T, he spells.

I wait.

Nothing.

T, he repeats.

He is waiting. He won't go on until I've got it. I feel waves of bitter frustration with myself. I hate not being able to do this. It feels as if I'm letting him down because my dense, befuddled brain can't make out what he is trying to tell me and this can only add to his already intense discomfort. We are getting perilously near the danger zone. That awful moment when the muddle and confusion ties us up in knots and frustration: and then Hasso gives up, stubbornly abandoning the attempt altogether; either because it genuinely no longer matters, or because he just can't summon the strength and enthusiasm to keep trying. I hate that. It's the worst of this whole business. When even the imperfect way we have of communicating lets us down and he's too weary to make an extra effort to get the message across. I know I have to be careful tonight. We're almost there, at the point when he'll cave in and give up because I'm not able to get the letters right. I shift my weight again, stretching my neck from side to side to get rid of the crick, and lean over the notepad.

I write out the letters again. I V E G O T T H E I N S R U + T, this time putting slashes between the letters at different places to make new words. I rearrange and realign them.

Suddenly I see it! The fog has lifted and it's as clear as day. I had left out the 'T'. Simple. Now it's so transparent. I also don't need the rest of the sentence because in spite of what he has said about guessing, my mind, now finally alert, starts to jump and somersault all the way to the end of his thought process.

I look up to him and smile. He is also smiling, or rather his face has twisted into that strange crooked expression that I have slowly come to recognise as a smile. His eyes are twinkling.

'The instructions! You've got the instructions!'

His eyes open wide.

'The instructions for Sophia!' I'm laughing now. I feel triumphant. It's the breakthrough. Suddenly, strangely, I'm not tired any more. He is willing me to go on. I know now he knows I understand. 'You've got the instructions to give Sophia about the rocket launcher!'

I realise that anyone overhearing this bizarre one-way exchange would think me quite touched. His eyes open wide and emphatically.

'She asked you today about that crazy thing you did in the army with the rocket launcher.' He blinks again. I've got it!

The crooked smile has widened. He's pleased and excited.

He's been thinking about that notoriously famous story of his feat while he was a soldier in the artillery during his military service. The children know the story of old and he never tires of telling it. Somehow or other, he accepted a challenge from his friends in the unit to get a rocket launcher to do a wheelie. Yes, a wheelie. Probably the result of some drunken bet. Not to be defeated, he put his mind to the task in all seriousness and managed to get the monstrous vehicle to roar across the yard on its back wheels, proving his friends wrong and winning the bet at the same time. He would always add with a chuckle, when he told the story, that his behaviour at the time was not exactly exemplary and that it wasn't long before his superior officers came rushing out to see what was going on. Incredibly, he managed somehow to make himself scarce and so escaped detection and a disciplinary. The wheelie incident, though, became something of a legend.

'She asked you how on earth you had done it . . .'

I TOLD HER I WOULD EXPLAIN

I laugh out loud. 'But she's only fourteen! She'll never understand. And when will she ever need instructions for how to do a wheelie with a rocket launcher?' He's laughing too now. That strange wide-mouthed open sound that comes up from his stomach.

I PROMISED

I shake my head, still laughing. 'You're incorrigible,' I tell him, bending down to kiss him.

He blinks firmly, holding his eyes tightly shut for a moment, which I now know has come to mean: 'I know.'

Then his eyes open and close rapidly, his sign that he wants to continue spelling.

LIEBE SOPHIA (Dear Sophia . . .) He always talks to the children in German and to me always in English.

I write the letters and know what's coming. It's going to be a whole letter to Sophia, probably full of hare-brained precise instructions about how to get a rocket launcher to do a wheelie. Looking up from the pad into his eager, insistent expression, I slowly lay down the pencil and shift my weight in the chair. I lean forward, letting my head move down towards his. The awkwardness of the position sends a sharp pain up my back. I feel his breath on my cheek and I kiss him again. I whisper in his ear, 'Can we do this tomorrow?'

His face still wears the same smile. 'Yes,' he blinks.

It's long after midnight. Straining forward in the chair to lower my head onto the pillow beside his, I close my eyes. The respite from the tiredness has only been momentary. When I open my eyes a few moments later he is still staring at me, the smile still hovering on his lips. I uncurl myself and sit up again.

'Thank you,' I say. 'Tomorrow, we'll do it tomorrow. I promise. She'll love it.'

My back is aching and the tiredness hurts. There are still all the drugs to do and the feeding through the tube to see to. Then I'll have to reposition him for a few hours' sleep so that he doesn't get too sore on one side, a difficult task that I'm only just learning to do unassisted by means of sliding sheets and brute force. It's really difficult and takes a lot out of me, and it has to be done several times a night.

But somehow tonight I don't mind. The truth is that I'd give everything just for that smile. It doesn't look much like the smile he gave me that first day we met, but in essence it is the same. The shared joy I feel to see it now even for that tiny, brief moment is worth all the hours of bleak exhaustion. Of course, before too long the smile will give way to the old despondency. It will fade all too quickly and the old coat will smother him again. Collar up, keeping the world, and me, out.

But tonight, as at so many other times, he has set aside his own pain. For a brief, precious moment he has been mine again. And I feel a strange lightness in my step as I turn away to get the medicines.

Several months later when finally home for good and with the aid of his new computer, the next day's message spelt out over several hours turned into a full-blown letter to Sophia with precise instructions for the rocket launcher wheelie. They contain detailed guidance, including the number of seconds to run the motor on full power before engaging the gear and a cautionary postscript suggesting that she shouldn't try to follow the instructions at a later date! It's signed 'I love you. Your Pappi.' It hangs on her wall to this day.

My Little Holiday

A pleasant surprise greeted us on our return to the hospital. Now that all the decorating had been done, we had all been moved back onto our original ward and I had been allocated a single room. This was much better than I had expected, and, although small, it was at least fairly private, away from the busy hub of the ward on a corridor approaching it. There was no one on this ward who was not wheelchair-bound, and the normal practice was to wheel all the patients into one central area during the day, so that staff could keep an eye on them. I always dreaded being parked in the main arena and being left there for hours on end, with nothing to do but observe the sad state of my fellow patients. Fortunately, Catherine's constant presence meant that this hardly ever happened to me, but I saw with horror how all the others had to endure it day after day. As we crossed the day area together, I couldn't help but glance at them all. With stoic calmness, they would wait their turn to be dragged away by a therapist eager for a session.

I was developing a rather macabre sense of humour as time went on and this always reminded me of a terrible story I had heard about a group of Americans during the Second World War. They had been shot down or shipwrecked (I can't quite remember which) in shark-infested waters somewhere in the Pacific. They instinctively swam tightly together for comfort and safety. This kept at least some lucky ones in the centre away from the hungry sharks, which rapidly gathered around them. However, realising that this was quite unfair, they took it in turns to occupy the outer edges of the circle, thus all sharing the risk of the fatal location on the outside. The gruesome masters of the deep returned again and again to drag the doomed to face their inevitable fate. Advancing greedily, these dreadful predators probably could not believe their luck. After all, how often did they find themselves surrounded by such rich pickings? The ordeal continued for what must have seemed like an eternity, with the only let-up coming when the merciless fish, with their cold, emotionless eyes, took a break from the feeding frenzy. The horror only ceased when the remaining men were rescued. My lurid imagination, contemplating the fate of the patients left to sit out their entire existence grouped in a circle like that, waiting for the next attack from a well-meaning therapist, couldn't help suggesting parallels with these desperate men, adrift in those shark-infested waters. Both sets of victims seemed to me equally helpless, and, indeed, hopeless.

Arriving back on the ward with so many more weeks ahead of me was not a pleasant prospect, but was at least made a little easier by the fact that we had proved that living at home was possible. Once things had been altered accordingly, I was sure that it would be better than trying to endure the alternative.

At around about this time, I contracted my first chest infection. My already severe difficulties with breathing increased tenfold and the nights became particularly horrendous. Alarmed, my doctor decided to get me checked at another hospital, so I was packed off for 'a few days', which, as is the way of things, turned into two weeks.

The journey to this hospital was much more difficult for Catherine, involving trains and buses each day, and taking two hours at least each way. Still, this did not deter her and she continued to come every single day and stay all day. At the weekends the children came with her and passed the time there as best they could. This was a really enormous hospital, but no one quite seemed to know what to do with me or where I actually belonged. They had put me on an ENT ward (probably because the specialist enlisted to explore my breathing problems was an ENT man), but this meant that the staff had absolutely no experience of a case like mine, and openly confessed themselves to be at a loss as to how to look after me. I was not too surprised, given the rarity of my condition. Indeed, I was touched by their honesty and by their very real endeavours to do their best for me. Transferring me from the bed to my wheelchair, for example, was a major problem for them. They had great difficulty tracking down a sling and a hoist and no one seemed to know where to start. A total of seven people were needed to accomplish this task. At first a little reticent with the staff in this new place, and, trusting to their knowledge and experience, Catherine held back and didn't want to intervene. After a few very uncomfortable attempts at hoisting, however, she offered to help and they soon learned to manage with just four people.

They were also brave enough to respond to our request for a shower on a regular basis, as they actually had shower trolleys there, but again this sometimes proved to be a case of the blind leading the blind. In spite of these difficulties, however, they soldiered on and several nurses and care assistants showed a touching willingness to acquire the knowledge and skills it took to help me.

The doctor in charge decided to conduct a 'sleep test' on me. This involved having a large mask fitted over my face all night long, which was designed to pump extra air into me at regular intervals. Then readings were taken in order to provide the doctors with data. At least that was the general idea. To seal the constant flow, albeit on the lowest setting, the mask was applied with the most incredible pressure. The research assistant who set up this instrument of torture, late at night after Catherine had left, literally resorted to brute force to make it fit snugly and, as she had never even seen me before, she had no idea of how to communicate with me. She solved this little problem very efficiently by simply ignoring me, and all the eye blinks in the world failed to alert her to the fact that, within seconds, I was finding the pain unbearable. Once her equipment was set up, she left me there to face the long interminable night. Not only was the pressure of the mask itself so painful, but the regular airflow pumping into me made me feel, in a strangely perverse way, as though I was suffocating. As the night progressed into the small hours, the nightmare reality of this situation became more and more intense. 'I don't believe it,' I muttered away silently in my mind, 'this can't be happening.' But happening it was, and it proved to be one of the most dreadful hospital experiences I have ever had. On the odd occasion when a nurse did pop her head round the door, she never tried to find out whether I was OK or not, but simply took note of the fact that I was still there, probably still alive and hadn't done a runner. I had had a few hospitalisations in my otherwise healthy life, usually as a result of accidents while doing sport, but this was worse than breaking my nose or even my cartilage problems. At least then I had been one of the walking wounded. The fruitless exercise was finally terminated around three to four in the early morning. It was decided that the readings were incon-clusive and Catherine was told to repeat the whole process on my next home visit and return the kit, so the readings could be taken again. She was horrified by what had happened. When we actually got round to doing this on my short weekend home visit, she set it up and watched me. She switched it all off after about ten minutes because she couldn't bear to see me suffer like that. When she told the hospital, they said that it was unlikely that they would get any dependable readings with me anyway. Personally I thought they might have suspected that all along.

Apart from the sleep test which, by the way, left a deep bruise and an open sore on my forehead to tell the tale for weeks afterwards, my stay at this hospital was a long-winded waiting game. I had virtually no access to physiotherapy and nothing to occupy my day for two whole weeks except Catherine's presence and her attempts to read to me or to distract me in any way she could think of. And that was becoming increasingly difficult for the two of us in a sterile room with just four walls and hours and hours of just sitting or lying there.

Finally, a rescue party was sent out in the form of one of my occupational therapists, who, once she realised what was going on, managed to hasten my orderly retreat back to rehab.

A final visit from the sleep test team pronounced that I had breathing difficulties at night, due to the stroke, and that these were exaggerated by my asthma, by the problems with my tongue, and by my recent chest infection. Surprise, surprise. At least they now had a medical term to classify this diagnosis. I was suffering from 'sleep apnoea'. This basically means that, when I do manage to fall asleep, I have great difficulty with noisy, obstructed airways and sometimes even stop breathing. This makes me wake up, gasping for air every fifteen minutes or so. In real terms, the result is total insomnia.

So, that was that. My little holiday was over. I couldn't help thinking that some people get to spend their fortnight's holiday on a warm beach, soaking up the sun. At least I was different.

Snow

One year it snowed so much that the grass in the field opposite our house disappeared beneath a blanket of white. The snow was knee-deep, the sky unbelievably high and blue. Hasso can never stay inside on such days. With vigorous digging, he cleared the snow from the front drive and piled it up on the lawn. When he came back into the house I touched the cold on his cheeks as he kissed me and his hair felt chilled with the freezing air.

'Let's go for a walk,' he said. 'There's so much snow and there's hardly anyone about yet. Let's go across the fields.'

So I grabbed a coat and wrapped Lucia up in layers of warm clothing. He lifted her up onto his shoulders and we set off. The air was sharp with cold but the sun was shining with intense brightness in a cloudless sky and it was wonderful to walk away from the house towards the woods in that crisp blue whiteness. Our feet crunched on the surface of the newly fallen snow and there was a beautiful stillness in the air.

We walked all the way to the edge of the woods before we met a man out with his dog. Hasso exchanged pleasantries with him and we continued on into the dark shadow of the tall trees. It was much colder along the woodland path and I could see the sun beckoning beyond the edge of the wood. I was relieved when Hasso suggested we cut across to get out into the sunlight again. We crossed the large field that in summer had been filled with swaying rye and had to lift our legs high to avoid the snow getting into our boots. It was hard work. Lucia was tired and was beginning to nod off on Hasso's shoulders. We rejoined the path and made our way home.

When we got back to the house, he lifted the now sleeping Lucia down and into my arms, saying, 'You go on in, I've got something to do.'

I took her in and put her to bed for a nap. The warm house felt almost tropical after the chill outdoors. As I came back into the kitchen I looked outside to see if I could see where Hasso was. He wasn't in the garden, front or back; but then I spotted him in the field opposite. He was jumping up and down in the snow. At first I couldn't make out what on earth he was doing and for a moment thought he'd simply got carried away, like a child intoxicated by excitement in the snow. But the look I saw on his face in the distance was serious and determined. With both feet together he was jumping up and down in the deep snow, bending his knees and springing up and forward. Moreover, there seemed to be a definite method in his madness. His jumps were regular and equally spread. He seemed to be measuring and calculating them and planning the next jump with considered precision. I was mystified. Not that I was unaccustomed to his often crazy moments of spontaneity, but this time I truly couldn't make out what on earth he was doing. He kept changing direction, sometimes leaping forward an enormous distance and then starting the erratic jumping once again.

I watched him for ages, completely puzzled and bemused. He seemed to be moving slowly across the field as if following some pattern laid out in the snow. I couldn't understand what he was up to. Then suddenly, as if he sensed that I was watching him, he stopped and turned in my direction. He was out of breath and panting. There was a broad smile lighting up his face and he was glowing. He began gesticulating to me to open the window. He called out to me from the middle of the field and his voice rang out in the chill clarity of the snowy air. 'It's for you!' he shouted, oblivious to anyone who might be listening nearby. He pointed to the upstairs window and signalled for me to go up and look.

I raced up the stairs. It crossed my mind as I went up that this life with him was a daily discovery. He was capable of surprising me each day, of propelling me towards another new encounter with him at each turn, and that I might never know the edges of him, the whole of him. Perhaps I would never discover the end of it. I wasn't at all sure that I ever wanted to either. Within his solid, strong, protective nature was a wild unpredictability. And it was that that I loved so much. The knowing, yet not knowing. Not all.

I flung open the windows of the bedroom and the rush of cold air took my breath away. But not nearly as completely as what I saw laid out in the blank whiteness before me.

Stretched out right across the surface of the snowy field, in letters all of six feet high, were the nine letters of my name.

Pillow Talk

A question began to bother me quite a bit at this stage. Back on the ward, the sleep problems that had plagued me since the stroke continued unabated. How on earth was this happening to me? How could someone who could normally fall asleep at the drop of a hat have developed such chronic sleep problems? In the army I had even been known to nod off when holding up the rear as last man on a summer night march, and could be perfectly happy and content to drift into the land of nod lying on tied-up, twisted rolls of razor wire, stacked in the frozen snow with temperatures somewhere in the region of −7°C. Also, I had never had a problem with snoozing away the tedium of long journeys by plane or ferry. Rather more embarrassingly, I had been known to doze off in comfortable chairs in the presence of certain dinner guests, and even that gentle kick under the table couldn't prevent me from doing so on some occasions.

So what could all this mean? I had certainly never had to count sheep in my life before. Yes, there had been all the broken nights suffered since February 1984 because of wakeful children and long hours in the office, but that becomes a part of life. I realised that the stroke was obviously to blame for the greater part of my problems with sleep, but I also began to think that the hospital environment and the feeding regime were making things a whole lot worse.

In particular, it was that liquid night feed, which goes directly into your stomach, and which you can't actually feel, but which still causes unwelcome stimulation, making you alert and preventing rest. The noise of the pump right next to you running all night is also disturbing. I started to put two and two together and came up with the idea that my other big problem at night – the plague of full body spasms – was actually connected. I remembered the advice I had once been given by an old Devon farmer and which I had always followed. If you want to get a good night's sleep, never go straight to bed after a visit to the pub. I surmised that the violent reaction set off by any bladder function was preventing me sleeping for more than thirty minutes at the most at a stretch. This was because the feed was set up to run over a ten-hour period at night, and, as it slowly filled my stomach, it was activating the bladder on a regular half-hourly basis. Such are the delights of liquid nourishment mixed with loads of water.

Clearly, the only way to get round this was to alter the feeding regime, but there was no way that this was going to be attempted until I came home from hospital, because it would mean rethinking the individual needs of all the patients on a ward like mine, and it is so much easier to hook all the patients up to a slow feeding pump at night. Mind you, a case could be made for seeing such changes as financially viable. Indeed, considering the small number of people involved, there must be definite advantages to be had from reducing the nauseating tiredness, which seems to run like a red thread through cases of patients with brainstem injury. Surely, less tiredness would mean more effective therapy, and this in turn would shorten the whole recuperation process, which is already long enough.

My main problem was that, once woken, I had a lot of difficulty in getting back to sleep again. So I lay motionless for many hours, with my eyes closed, thus involuntarily deceiving the nurses on duty who hovered like ghosts from bed to bed. Basically, my 'shut-eye' policy was no more than a kind of scanning of the inner eyelids, because, although I was awake, I was trying desperately to grab at least forty winks, and knew that at least acting as if I was asleep might increase any chances of some kind of sleep. However, quite apart from the feeding tube problems, even a doze, or what my father-in-law used to call 'ein Kip', was really out of the question, because once a night nurse popped her head round the door and asked if I was asleep, I had had it, and was wide awake until the next night.

The tiredness was not just a case of struggling with sleepiness. It tended to impact on my whole body and increased the muscle tone in my limbs quite steeply, making me very stiff indeed. Moreover, continuous yawning can exacerbate the spasms, which in turn can leave your body awkwardly contorted in a painful position. In my case, the full body spasms gradually started to recede post-Christmas 2001, but they have never left me. I still suffer from them on a daily basis, but like to think that improvement on this front is, perhaps, at least the first indication of healing that could be directly attributed to the area affected by the stroke – if, of course, brain tissue can possibly regenerate against all the odds. This would be significant in itself. It was not surprising, though, that the weaker the full body spasms became, the better I managed to sleep ... which looks suspiciously like the proof of the pudding to me.

For the time being, however, I had to be satisfied with relying on the occasional involuntary catnap during the quieter periods of the day, which was usually induced by the strong medication I was under. I can tell you that I still long for the opportunity to listen to my pillow, uninterruptedly, for a whole night. The truth is, though, that from this point on, the benefits of a full night's sleep were to remain for me a thing of the past.

Since I couldn't swallow properly I had been fed through tubes since the day of the stroke. An amount of around 2000 calories was being pumped into me per day through my tube. This was, of course, totally adequate, but it did nothing to assuage my desire for real food and provided no sensation at all in terms of taste. It is an absolute myth, by the way, that I have nameless, rare taste buds somewhere in my stomach that can appreciate this sort of canned calories. The only reason I get to taste it at all is because some of it always comes up again, without fail, leaving a sour and unpleasant burning sensation in my mouth and throat. A food additive without a European Directive! When I couldn't bear this hideous, lingering brew any longer, I got Catherine to ask my doctor if anything could be done to prevent this reaction. I then received some medication to act as an antidote, but was perplexed to discover that this remedy only worked occasionally. If it worked, then I experienced a strange taste which reminded me of Pastis. Sometimes the whole experience felt like an unnerving game of pinball, with the irrepressible liquid coming up again and again for another shot ... 'Tilt, game over, last player shoots again'. After some time, I noticed that this medication only achieved the desired effect when administered last, after all the other ones had been given. It therefore seems to follow one of my infallible rules for liquids consumed rather too enthusiastically at drinking sessions, the so-called LiFo principle ('Last in, First out'). The trouble was, the 'o' bit was rather an unpleasant hurdle, often resulting in full-scale vomiting. No joke when you can't move.

After losing so much weight in my critical stage, which had lasted weeks and weeks, I began to put it on again as soon as I stabilised, and one of the distinct disadvantages of this type of feeding soon became apparent to me. It is very difficult to get the planning for calorie consumption right for a patient like me. At the beginning, I rapidly acquired a spare tyre, which gradually assumed the shape of an overdue pregnant oyster, while the rest of me continued to waste away. My spare tyre was dubbed 'Emperor Joe' by my inventive son to complement his own mini version named 'Master Joe'. It wasn't long, however, before that disappeared too.

Calories, ah calories ... my notions of calories now rest entirely in my memory and my frequent dreams. I will admit here that my reputation for being able to eat almost anything was actually only slightly exceeded by my willingness to drink almost anything ... in rather large amounts, and whenever the occasion demanded. It was nothing new to people who knew me before this that I was quite happy to finish off the wine at a dinner party, or even to polish off what was left of the whisky, once a bottle had been opened and shared with friends. To be quite honest I would have preferred any of those, even in a stale or acidic state, to this nasty concoction seeping up my throat. It could always have been worse, I suppose. After all, poor old Socrates had been forced to drink bitter poison from his cup. On the other hand, I sometimes felt that wouldn't have been such a bad thing, after all, if only I had been able to drink it in the first place.

The dramatic effects of a stroke are pretty visible to everyone, I suppose, but what a lot of people don't notice are the many, many side effects which carry on down the years making life more and more uncomfortable. Perhaps it is high time I had a real moan about a few such 'minor irritations' which, in truth, are a fairly subtle kind of torture. Maybe it will do me good to get a few of these off my chest.

One such small problem for me is the cold, and I seemed to feel it even more in my new room throughout the months of January and February. I realised that I would never even be able to make it to the first threshold of Maslow's famous Hierarchy of Needs, because I could not achieve one of the most basic 'needs' of all, which is just to be able to keep warm. Whenever anybody came into my room, they invariably commented on how warm it was in there, and often proceeded to fling open a window, retreating with the door wide open behind them for what I can only assume they thought was my benefit. Since the stroke, due to the poor circulation in my body, I am actually freezing cold most of the time, even on a warm day. The problem in hospital, particularly at night, was that once someone had opened a window, they tended to forget to come back and close it again. Sometimes, judging my room to be too warm, they even removed my one precious blanket and left me freezing for hours under the sheet with the window wide open. My solution to this was to try, by means of vigorous eye blinks, to indicate that I didn't actually want the window opened in the first place. Hardly anyone ever took any notice of my frantic efforts. On reflection, I suppose that many members of staff didn't understand my silent efforts at communication, and, because I couldn't speak to them probably assumed I was fine. However, the fact remained that no matter how hard I tried to get the message across, I still had to spend night after night shivering until the morning. Incidentally, I really couldn't work out why they were so keen to remove blankets and leave windows open in the first place. I have never heard of anyone dying of stale air, while, on the other hand, thousands have unceremoniously kicked the bucket by freezing to death. Indeed, I have now become so sensitive to the cold that, once there is a draught anywhere, no amount of wrapping me up like a mummy will help. I seem to be able to feel the cold crawling up the inside of my arms and down my spine.

So, apart from all the obvious disadvantages of a stroke, there are all the traditional irritations, which in another life might appear fairly trivial, but in my situation have a way of becoming quite unbearable. That little itch, for example, which refuses to go away, and which you obviously can't scratch. What I wouldn't give sometimes to be able to banish the itch with the tiniest of gestures, before it builds and builds, eventually sending me into paroxysm of spasms and still doesn't go away until someone notices and will scratch it for me. I found myself musing that the stroke had been rather like a classic case of getting two, or three, or even many more, for the price of one. Like one of those special offers you can't refuse, no purchase necessary, no postage or package costs, plus the added bonus of an unexpected delivery.

One such little extra is the lack of muscle control in my mouth. This has resulted in my being unable to control my tongue, or to prevent saliva dribbling down my chin and onto my clothing. If that isn't bad enough, I have the additional problem of the rather dangerous impulse, or rather reflex, to bite down on anything inside or even near my mouth, including my own tongue and cheek.

Any attempts of the speech therapists to get small amounts of yoghurt down me were invariably hindered by the relentless onslaught of my old, by now quite worn-down teeth. They clamped down, as usual, at the slightest stimulus, callously demanding their 'pound of flesh'. This normally consisted of chunks out of my own cheeks, tongue or lips, and occasionally raised shrieks of pain from well-meaning therapists. I struggled to swallow the copious amounts of my own blood trickling down my throat, and must have looked like a relative of Count Dracula, as the remainder left a trail at the side of my mouth and dripped down my chin onto my shirt. I sometimes felt like an honorary Maasai warrior, living mostly on a diet of milk and blood. It might be of interest to note that I sometimes had more swallowing success with rather bland food, as long as it was blended to a soft pulp. I could manage a few spoonfuls of that without it activating the saliva glands too much, and making it all too watery and difficult to swallow. When this did happen, as it all too often still continues to do, it resulted in huge coughing fits and anyone within a few feet of me ended up being splattered with yoghurt, or whatever pulp they were trying to make me swallow. My children would even dive out of range, in exaggerated panic, shouting, 'Take cover!' My continual efforts to improve my swallow have not had a great deal of success and this very basic function – something, incidentally, that I had never consciously paid much attention to in my life before – has always remained a source of great difficulty for me on a daily basis. I have never been able to chew or swallow, or really to control my tongue at all. I continue to keep trying each day, but have never managed much more than a glorified gulping. As a result, and to my great disappointment, I am still dependent on my PEG tube for food and liquids. In truth, I still long for the taste and texture of real food and drink and am daily tormented by their perpetual absence.

When you find yourself robbed of all muscle control, and a victim of incontinence in particular, perhaps one of the most difficult things to bear is the total lack of personal privacy. It's as if the slightest wishes for modesty have somehow been handed in at reception along with your coat and gloves upon arrival. Consequently, no one seems to think that they are at all important to you any more. The real truth of the matter is that it never gets any easier to have all and sundry poking you around and handling your body like a piece of public property. Gone are all the boundaries and the privacy that you have nurtured all your life, without which it's hard to feel very human. Privacy is now, sadly, only a memory. Each day brings new tortures of this kind, and embarrassment, though ever present, becomes redundant, because no one notices how you feel about it anyway. Catherine knows how I feel about this and she has always been hugely protective; but, of course, there is very little she can do to change how things are and what needs to be done to me each day. Even taking over large areas of these responsibilities herself has not made me feel a lot of better about being so helpless, though it has gone some way to reducing a little of the embarrassment.

Then, of course, there is the daily problem of stifling one's frustration at not being able to talk, not even being able to make the slightest meaningful sound that could alert those around you to that recurring itch, for example, or to your need to communicate the pain in your shoulder or legs. Not to mention that all-embracing and enduring desire to tell those you love how you feel and what they mean to you. Stringing single letters into words and then into sentences, however, is not only incredibly hard work for me and for anyone trying to decipher my eye blinks, but is also horribly long-winded and tedious. Much of my life and my interaction with people have been, I realise, so much a question of dialogue. I am very talkative and very playful with language, and have often been teased about my tendency to invent and even corrupt words just for fun. It feels like exchanging a rapid-firing machine gun for a cumbersome single-shot musket. It is difficult to rein in galloping thoughts and to stop your eyelids closing of their own accord. This results in mistakes with letters, and sometimes even whole words go missing, thus throwing confusion into any attempt to communicate. In addition, when I am using the single switch to operate the computer to type my messages (and also this book), corrections themselves are a time-consuming and frustrating business. Especially when I only manage to see the cursor about ten per cent of the time.

My problems weren't helped much by the fact that I have frequent attacks each day of what I call the shakes, the medical term for it being 'clonus'. My legs, from below the knees down to my feet, begin to shake uncontrollably until someone applies gentle pressure to them the other way.

A really annoying thing that often happened to me at night, after Catherine had hit the road to return to Kent, was to do with the routine of the night staff. Once I could feel comfortable with watching TV, Catherine frequently left me watching something when she went home, to help me pass the time. Often a nurse or care assistant would come in as part of the ward routine and switch on the light behind me to replace the overhead lighting. This was fine, but at about 9 p.m., when the night staff had arrived to take over, I would begin to wonder whether or not they would remember to switch it off when they turned off the TV. Each time this was a bit of a gamble. It was, frankly, pot luck for me whether I had to spend the entire night trying to sleep under a bright light, or whether I would be treated to the faint glow of the night lighting on the ward. There were actually so many incidents when the light was left on that I lost count.

There was an additional problem to this. A call-alarm system had been rigged up for me on one of the night splints I had to wear on my arms, allowing me to press an ultra-sensitive switch with the tiny single movement left to me in my right thumb, and thus to summon help should I need it. That was the idea, anyway. I was to find out to my peril that when I actually needed help during the night, there were problems with the wiring of the whole system. For a while, I thought the system must be faulty, for, try as I might, I couldn't make the alarm go off. Catherine always made me test it for her before leaving, and would only go when she was satisfied that it worked and that I would be able to summon help during the long night hours. That, after all, was the whole purpose of the thing. It was ages before the connection was made with the overhead light. The technical staff who had set it up came to the ward and showed genuine concern over my predicament. They made several adjustments and everyone crossed their fingers that this would sort the problem out. However, unbeknown to me, or anyone else for that matter, interfering with the light switch also had the effect of disabling the call alarm. So, time and again, I either had to spend the entire night wired up to the alarm system, but under the glare of what felt like an interrogation lamp, because no one had remembered to turn the light off, or lie in relative darkness with my legs bent up, desperately trying to get the alarm to work, so that someone would come and unfold them to get me out of my agony. I couldn't bear to face it, but I knew that for the whole duration of those long night hours, there would be no means of calling for help.

I will readily admit that on many occasions it was quite impossible to hold back the tears. Curiously enough, my fragile emotional state was often exaggerated by the fact that certain physical stimuli also made tears come to my eyes, particularly during early morning stretches by the physio team. Later this actually reached a crescendo of three to four incidents every day, so that it became impossible for the casual onlooker to tell whether I was breaking my heart or whether I was just unable to control a physical reaction. Sometimes, frankly, it was both. These problems with hypersensitivity were rectified much later, though sadly only partially, through a course of acupuncture. This, interestingly enough, was the only thing that also worked to alleviate the hypersensitivity of my upper lip area, which had long been the culprit in making shaving and teeth cleaning such horrendous experiences. Unfortunately, we have never been able to find a cure for the terrible itching around my eyes, which is particularly bad in the early morning, and which can drive me mad when I am not able to attract Catherine's attention to it immediately.

Before I leave this particular grouching session behind, I would just like to say a word or two about tilt tables. Now, a tilt table is a kind of plinth on wheels that can be tilted electrically, to bring the patient lying on it up to a vertical position. This is all fine in itself, and, of course, as I was so often reminded by the physios, of obvious benefit to the Achilles tendons. As a species, I was told, we have evolved to stand and to walk, and not to be lying or sitting all day as I now was. My ankle joints were never getting the chance to stretch in the way they were designed to under the weight of my body, and were therefore shortening and causing me pain.

On the other hand, there were distinct disadvantages. Let me start in descending order, moving from the head down. First of all, my eyes could rarely make out the objects in front of me, because of the angle I ended up 'standing' in and the problems I have with my eye muscles. Added to this, it takes some adjusting to be suddenly elevated from the horizontal to the vertical, after spending most of your time on your back. Often my head would flop backwards, leaving me leaning back in the posture of a praying mantis, and so providing the added bonus of life without breathing, because, in that position, I could do nothing to stop my tongue falling backwards and blocking my airway. Gradually my body got used to being upright for short periods of time, though this had to be kept very brief in the first few months, as I had a habit of fainting clean away when finally 'standing'. As I am totally unable to hold myself erect, however, I tend to commence a slow slide as soon as I'm up, and end up slipping into a position resembling the leaning tower of Pisa. Then there was the tray, which was inserted quite high up under my arms to act as a kind of armrest. Unused by now as I was to having my arms elevated in this way, it was usually only a minute or two before this began to make them ache with a vengeance, and this soon became excruciating, particularly in the area between my elbow and shoulder, and on several occasions it made me pass out with the pain. It was assumed that these blackouts were due to circulation problems, which I had had on several occasions, but I knew that this felt different. I always passed out when the pain reached unbearable limits. Later, in fact, I asked them to remove the tray altogether and the fainting fits stopped. Unfortunately, this procedure contributed in no small way to the subluxation of my shoulder joints. I have often been teased about my long arms and I have even been affectionately compared to Lucky Luke, who, sitting astride his horse, Jolly Jumper, was famously able simultaneously to roll a cigarette and shoot his gun, 'faster than his own shadow'. Being on the tilt table was a bit like being on the rack, though, and my arms felt as if they were being stretched even longer.

Finally, certain physios sometimes showed concern for my heaving chest, but this probably originated from all my basic breathing difficulties. Quite embarrassingly, these breathing problems also seemed to bring on fits of yawning, but no one appeared to realise that these were not a sign of tiredness or boredom, but part of the chain reaction set off by lack of air. However, that didn't stop people asking me again and again 'Am I boring you?' or, even more irritatingly, 'Am I keeping you up?'

By the way, apropos of Achilles tendons, every time they were mentioned my eyes must have glazed over. I don't know what the physios must have thought, but just the mention of the name was enough. That was it, I was off ... on a completely different track, thousands of years and miles away, indulging fantasies and reminiscences of the *Iliad* and the *Odyssey*. On one particular morning, while they worked away, stretching and pulling at my ever-stiffening legs and arms, and as I stood in a kind of Christ-like pose above them all, visions of Troy, of sulky Achilles and his fellow besieging Greeks sped through my mind. The tragedy and high drama of someone so unlikeable overpowering Hector and dragging his body for nine days around the walls of Troy never failed to move me. While I mused on the fate of Hector and Achilles, I was reminded of Odysseus and the cunning Greek plan for infiltrating soldiers into Troy. I realised, with a sting of pain and pleasure, that the physios had no idea where my mind was travelling. Visions of wooden horses and muttered warnings of how not to trust Greeks bearing gifts would only have left them baffled, even if I had been able to speak the words.

Virtual travel had now indeed become my speciality, through space and time, and it wasn't long before thoughts of Odysseus turned to the Roman version of his name, Ulysses, and off I was again, musing on snippets I could remember about his nineteenth-century namesake, General Ulysses S. Grant, the commander of the Union Army in the American Civil War. One terrible story about Grant's men that I remembered illustrates the awfulness of war and always makes me quake when I hear the expression 'to lead someone up the garden path' or even the single dreadful word 'wilderness'. At one particular stage of the war, Grant led his troops into the heavy underbush of the Wilderness. Fighting began and, two days later, smouldering paper cartridges set fire to dry leaves. As far as I remember, around 200 wounded men were either suffocated or burned to death. Of the roughly 88,000 men that Grant took into the Wilderness, about 14,000 were casualties and 3,000 were reported missing.

My mind was clearly compensating for the tedium of real life by flights of memory and fantasy, as well as the occasional return to bits of history I happened to have read. Once launched there was often no stopping it. Thinking about Grant, I suddenly remembered his face on the front of the $50 bill and right there and then, so very clearly in my mind's eye, I could see, standing on the banks of the final stretches of the Hudson River, looking towards New Jersey, the national monument in New York that commemorates his name, just as I had seen it in the sunshine on my last trip to the Big Apple.

Little did the physios know how a session on the tilt table and that one reference to Achilles tendons had sparked off an odyssey of my very own that morning. My mind, my memories and all my fantasies were, at least, still very much my own.

'When I Come Home'

'When I come home, we'll swap rooms with Lucia and sleep on the ground floor.'

I look up from my paper, the pen hovering above the words. I'm unsure what to do or what to say. It's unclear from the words what he is suggesting. He knows full well that Lucia's room is far too small to take his enormous hospital bed and all his hoisting equipment. I don't for a moment think that he has forgotten that, or that he hasn't been thinking about this conversation for some time, preparing it in his mind while he has been lying in the wakeful darkness of the early hours in this hospital room. With all the economy of meaning pressed into our present mode of communication, I have learnt to look for shades of suggestion and to strain to read between the lines. But this has thrown me. I could ask him straight out what he means, but I'm slightly scared of the answer. The speed and determination of the introductory words have put me on my guard. I know that he's telling me much more than the mere words that have emerged on the page in front of me.

'As soon as Mum and Dad go home, Lucia will probably be more than happy to have our old room,' I say finally, looking intensely at him to try and detect what's in his mind. Then, looking down at the paper in order to avoid his eyes, the cop-out: 'There's not too much to do to convert the living room for your bed,' I add.

Slowly, he moves his head a fraction from side to side. This is a new movement. He has recently discovered that he can do this from time to time. It doesn't always work when he needs it and sometimes refuses to respond at all, but today he's managing it fine. He's determined to use it to make his point. He has anticipated resistance and is at pains to make sure I know exactly what he means.

The implication of what he's saying becomes all too obvious. He goes for absolute clarity, throwing down the gauntlet to me.

'We will use Lucia's room when I don't need the bed.'

The words pile up on the page and I feel the heat rising through my brain. Steering a course through this minefield is becoming increasingly difficult. The doctors have told me that if there is no real progress in his condition within the first year, it becomes highly unlikely (they don't say 'impossible' but I suspect that's what the words mean) that there will be any recovery at all. Effectively that means that the patient remains locked in until the end of their life. None of them has actually told Hasso this in so many words. I have so far not found the courage or the cruelty (I can't decide which I need) to tell him either. Not in so many words. But I know with the sort of uncanny certainty that comes from knowing someone so intimately that he has worked this out for himself. And I'm pretty certain that he knows better than I do that his body hasn't responded enough in the past nine months to give him real hope of recovery.

I am, however, seeing daily signs that he has decided to fly in the face of all this and espouse the only bearable stance possible. He seems to have decided that he will behave from now on as if his recovery is a reality which is both achievable and nothing less than a necessity. I suspect that it is perhaps more for our benefit than his own.

The intensity of his eyes fixed on mine wills me to suspend

the disbelief he knows I feel and to go along with him. I feel awkward and bitter. I know that it's not fair to him to encourage the fiction and yet I cannot bring myself to undermine this new determination. I suspect it is the only weapon he has left for dealing with the misery of it all. Self-delusion, I know all too well, is immensely powerful and can fuel self-belief, which in turn can produce a greater sense of well-being and can lead to God knows what miracles. I have no right to strip him of this, his last and only prop. In fact, I feel light-headed at the sheer strength of his determination. I am overwhelmed by the feeling that he has never been so close to madness and that I have never loved him more.

But the well of bitterness runs deep in me and it sticks in my throat to collude in this. The best I can do is force myself to a half-truth.

'OK, but first we have to concentrate on getting the living room ready for you when you come home.' He knows I'm side-stepping. I hate these mind games. He is already one step ahead of me.

It comes with a whiplash sting of audacity.

'I will walk' is his reply, shattering in its directness.

It's as much as I can do to keep the letters steady as my eyes begin to swim. If I wipe the tear away he will notice. It falls with a large plop onto the page, blurring and smudging the ink in the last line. When I finally summon the courage to look up at him, he is blinking his eyes. He wants to continue. The words come one after another, tipping out in quick succession, tumbling and falling onto the page.

'I am so sad all of the time,' he begins, 'but I am strong. You know that. I will never give up even though I want to. You and the children are everything to me. You will see. I can be so strong. Stronger than even you know.'

We are both crying now.

'Hold my hand,' he spells.

I sniff and wipe the tears away. I run my damp hand down his and wrap the fingers of his hand around mine. They are cold and the skin on his once rough and hard hands is now smooth and thin. He looks right into my eyes. Summoning all his will and every tiny ounce of strength left in him, slowly, incredibly, he squeezes my hand in his. It's only the lightest of pressure, only the whisper of a squeeze, but it is unbelievable. It is the most amazing sensation I have ever felt.

Stunned and speechless I look up into the clear blue pools of his eyes. His gaze is steady and unwavering. One single tear detaches itself from his left eye and runs down his cheek.

His eyes blink out the next words. No need to write them down.

'You see,' they say.

PART FOUR

Coming Home

March 2001

Into the Unknown

After all attempts at trying to fit me into an existing wheelchair had failed, we had to admit total defeat and a new one had to be tailor-made for me. This involved a 'matrix base' seating system, mounted on a frame, a structure which had been perfected in the hospital wheelchair department. This new chair was indeed very snug, but several alterations to it would be required to prevent pain building up in my legs and my stiff, old left arm and shoulder. These lay motionless and, seemingly, very calm in front of me, because, of course, they couldn't move independently when they began to hurt.

When, after months and months of waiting, the new chair finally arrived, Catherine and I were in the gardens of the hospital one day, when the label still hanging from the frame caught her eye. With utter disbelief she picked it up and read the details of the manufacturer to me. The frame had been built in a village in Devon, just outside the little town where we used to live. The words Farthing Lane were indeed much more than just a place name to me. During the many years we had lived in Devon, had I not walked down that hedge-lined country lane with the family at weekends, and driven hurriedly past it every day on my way to my office in Plymouth? Unless I managed to get stuck behind a milk lorry or a tractor, that journey was mostly a delight, especially on the wonderful, soft, Devon summer mornings. It certainly never felt like commuting does in the South East. Plymouth, the so-called windy city, has always felt to me somewhat like a European Chicago, only obviously on a smaller scale. All the wind and new buildings, just not so much high-rise. Plymouth is rightly proud of its nautical history and for its connections with its famous son, Francis Drake, who, when informed on the Hoe of the approach of the Spanish Armada, famously declared he would first finish his game of bowls and then finish off the Spaniards. Opposite the Hoe is an island which now bears his name, and I could clearly see both landmarks from my office window.

Just behind Farthing Lane lay Compton Castle, the home of Sir Humphrey Gilbert, the half-brother of Sir Walter Raleigh, another Devon man. This was yet another of the strange, tenuous links, weaving my new life in and out of my old one. From Plymouth to Compton to London ... all linked by a wheelchair. Apropos of Raleigh, of tobacco and potato fame, I often pictured him relaxing with a nice pipe, contemplating the smoke rising up from his newly discovered tobacco, unaware that he had returned from the New World with the future cat-o'-nine-tails of the modern age. Intriguingly enough, a Mexican friend of mine once told me that one of the most popular brands of cigarettes in Mexico to this day is still called Raleigh ... proving once again that fact is stranger than fiction.

My new wheelchair was fine enough, a big improvement on the other ones in fact, but there was still one problem. Since I am on the tall side, my long arms kept slipping right off the tray provided and, being dead weights, they would fall right down, often jerking my already painful shoulder joints. The staff in the OT and wheelchair department came up with the idea of fitting extensions onto the side of the chair so that this would not happen. This particular wheelchair was, however, already very big, and adding any more to the width would make it impossible for me to get through the doors at home. While the team was pondering a solution, my cousin, who lives in England, arrived to visit me. He had come to see me on several occasions in hospital, and often pops in for a visit now I am at home. He got interested in the problem and suggested a hinged, flap-like set of wings on a slim-lined tray, which could be held in place by bolts. The team was delighted with the idea and pronounced him good enough to be an engineer, which, of course, is what he is. The wings were a great idea. Indeed, they proved to be the perfect solution for preserving our door frames at home intact.

In the meantime, the OTs and the IT department had started to make significant progress in harnessing some areas of communication technology for my use. This was to be one of the biggest breakthroughs for me. The main problem has always been the very limited amount of movement left to me – still only a little in my right hand, but not enough to serve any practical purpose. Consequently, although there is ample material in terms of software for computer programmes that are designed to assist communication in the physically disabled, I have huge difficulties accessing any of it. That is mainly because I can't use a mouse at all. Finally, though, a system was devised for me using a single switch and an on-screen keyboard scanner. If I was able to use the tiny movement in my thumb to click at the right time, I could select letters as the computer scanned them, and so begin to write text. This was a painfully slow and laborious process, particularly for someone who, as a normal part of a busy schedule, had been used to using computers for speed-writing reports and departmental business, either in the office, or on laptops on planes or in hotels. However, it did mean a great deal in terms of liberation from the walls of silence that held me in. Letter by agonisingly slow letter I started to create words and sentences. At first I was only able to use the equipment in the

IT department during my 40-minute therapy session and usually managed only a word or two. In time, however, I was allowed to borrow a laptop for use in my room and, when I went home at the end of January for my birthday weekend, was allowed to take it with me.

With the help of this system I began to take part a tiny bit more in the alteration plans and was able to suggest a few ideas for all the work. I knew that, for the first time, a major alteration project at home would have to go ahead without any real input from me. Very hard to swallow, as I had always been very active at home on the DIY front. The alterations would leave only a small front room to be converted into the family sitting room, as we didn't have a lot of space to play with. Now I would have to let Catherine carry the burden of organising this all alone, although the actual hard graft would obviously have to be done by builders and helpful friends and family. Since it involved transforming our living room into our bedroom and serious building work along the way, I did find it helpful to be able at least to contribute some ideas.

By the time my stay in rehab was entering its sixth month, with only a nine-month stay in total envisaged for me, it became startlingly clear that we would have to plan for the future. All our hopes of a rehabilitation stay that would restore at least a modicum of independence to me had clearly been too naïve, for, in the early days after the stroke, we could not have known the terrible truth we were now beginning to glimpse ... that things would, in essence, be no better one year on. The options were bleak to say the least. I could only judge my chances by the other cases similar to mine that I had come across in the hospital – and there were only three others in the whole time I was there. One had slowly got a little better, one had died before the allotted time was up, and the other had experienced virtually no improvement. The message was really loud and clear, but incredibly painful for us both to swallow. I had not died and was not getting better. The future for such as me was not exactly buzzing with options. It turned out that, although I had been permitted home leave, no one was seriously contemplating home as a permanent option. Long-term residential care, a nursing home, was the only thing under discussion. As soon as Catherine got wind of this, her long-felt, long-repressed horror burst to the surface. She told everyone that under no circumstances was such a possibility to be considered and that there was to be no argument whatsoever. I was going home. That was that. Huge efforts were made to persuade her that this was not a good idea and that she wouldn't be able to cope. She disagreed, and told them all quite firmly that a young man of forty-three, a husband and father, needed to be at home with his family. There was, basically, no other option imaginable.

Needless to say, the difficulties of this decision were to be almost insurmountable, and they began well before I left hospital. Catherine realised that if we were to get no help from the state (either financial or practical), then we would have to get our act together quickly and hurry the building alterations along, so that the house would at least be ready for me when my time in hospital was up.

Frankly, I believe that our situation highlighted the enormity of an illusion we had long shared. We were only just beginning to realise how naïve we had been. For some reason, we had somehow always thought that we were protected by what we imagined was some kind of safety net for those unlucky enough to have their lives smashed by illness and unforeseen events. We were, of course, to discover that the system works fine, until something really extreme goes wrong, and then you begin to come unstuck.

Our attitude in the face of this was one that sometimes

shocked people. I was never present at the discussions Catherine had with the bodies concerned, but, from what she told me, it seems that she had to fight her corner on more than one occasion. Her position became hardened as the friendly advice became more negative. She explained that if residential care was the only option they would support, then we would have to go it alone. Effectively, she felt that the reluctance to help us was tantamount to letting us fall right off the edge of the world, as, from now on, we would have to fight every step of the way to achieve basic standards of care for me. Whatever the result, she was not going to let the preferred options and easy solutions push me into a future I didn't want. Frankly, she felt that very few people had any conception of how hard things were going to be for us. We had a good idea that we were taking on the near impossible, but a little more help and support from the system would certainly have eased the load a bit. Indeed, having paid into the system for so many years, was it unreasonable to look for help from the safety net we had presumed was there?

In the long run, after numerous meetings, Catherine was able to convince the decision-makers that there was no point in discussing residential care or nursing homes with us any more. Eventually, arrangements began to go ahead for a discharge from hospital to home. The planned support levels at home, however, were still absolutely minimal, and she had to cope virtually alone at home for more than a year, before things began to improve significantly. Apart from the morning visits of nurses three times a week and an hour or so's help each day from carers to assist with the essential jobs of showering and dressing, etc., this applied to all aspects of the life we were proposing at home, from my need for continuing physiotherapy to adaptations of the home and many other issues. The task was daunting to say the least. One thing was sure. Going solo certainly meant we would have to start organising the transfer to home as soon as possible, because, judging by Catherine's early efforts at getting things rolling, we realised that we were going to have one almighty battle on our hands.

I suppose the main problem for the powers that be and their legions of bureaucrats was that, when confronted by an attitude like ours, they didn't really know how to cope. The truth is that neither of us has ever had much time, or respect for that matter, for red tape. Catherine was clearly under a lot of strain by now, but was not going to give up. At times I was reminded of the story of Alexander the Great when faced with the famous Gordian knot. Unable to unravel it, he simply got out his sword and cut right through it.

Anyway, stuck there in hospital, I had very different battles to fight, although these at times tended to feel more like tilting at windmills.

Without the enormous support and leverage of one other person in those early stages, however, the battle would no doubt have been tougher. Our local MP, now a good friend, had received a letter from Catherine outlining the desperate plight we were in and asking for support. He wasted no time in responding and in intervening on our behalf in the long battle ahead, wherever he felt it feasible. His constant efforts and advocacy over time have edged the local health authority, step by step, closer to improving the provision for me at home, which at that stage (in terms of medical and practical help) was close to zero. It is no exaggeration to say that his intervention actually helped to ensure that I would be able to come home when I did. At the very time we needed a strong ally, who was a 'doer' and not just a talker, his help proved invaluable.

We decided to get the alterations done as a top priority, and as we had already discovered from our encounters with Social Services, very little help would be forthcoming on that front. Catherine had already contacted the builders to do the basic alterations (taking down walls and replacing windows, etc.). But the race was now on to find one that would be able to start the job and get it done before my discharge date. This was to prove nigh on impossible, as most seemed to have enough work for the next six months. Finally, though, she found a team that would do at least some of the work in time, and we now decided it was time to think laterally.

We turned to our only fixed assets ... friends and family. As soon as they got to know about our dilemma, the response was amazing. The group that came together for four wet days in February 2001 soon came to be referred to in the family as the 'A Team'. They all co-ordinated annual leave from work and travel arrangements to be able to come. They pooled tools and DIY know-how and, in just four days, turned a large piece of sloping lawn in our back garden into a level brick terrace, flush with the new raised doorway to my bedroom (our former living room), and a ramp to join front to back gardens. They even managed to down tools one night and travel up to central London to visit me showing me 'before and after' photos of the operation. They also made much of teasing me that there I was, in a dry, warm bed, snug as a bug in a rug, while they were slaving away exposed to all the elements. The weather was certainly not kind to them and the early darkness meant that they had to rig up a spotlight to continue working into the evenings, in order to get it all done in the allotted time. Their organised and tidy approach to the job provided endless entertainment for my parents-in-law, who found the whole enterprise very inspiring. Our neighbours called them 'the heavy mob', as they laboured away at the normally harmless clay soil, which the downpours had changed into soapy clods as heavy as a ton of bricks. But their efforts really did make me take heart, because I could now finally see an end in sight to my own version of *Waiting for Godot* in this place and it was very touching to feel their dedication.

Before I can let them totally disappear and allow everyone to fade into oblivion, there are a few facts that ought to be related about the amazing friends and relations who made up the A Team. They were more like a UN task force really, as they came from all over, and the languages spoken between them (but not necessarily in use all the time) included English, German, Spanish, Serbian, Russian and French. Some of them had never met before this, but they forged strong and happy friendships, which have endured, and they proved that the pooling of many talents works well. They had lots of laughs together, and actually finished the job on time. Their success inspired them to come together again later in the year, when I was already home, to do another demolition job on our kitchen in order to provide extra access for me. Their overall contribution literally made it possible for me to get in and out of the house in the wheelchair, which was a *sine qua non* of my coming home, and the construction of this large terrace was to give me the additional benefit of a kind of open-air room for the summer.

The work on the terrace and improvements for accessing the garden were later completed by a new set of amazing friends, who came to my rescue in the village and who have since transformed my life in every sense of the word. Eventually they took over the role of the A Team and provided countless improvements for me, including a huge path throughout the garden, so my wheelchair could get round, and alterations to provide a room for physio equipment, training and IT, plus many other kindnesses too numerous to mention here. Their energies, dedication and huge efforts have often overwhelmed me and I have come to feel a deep and abiding affection for them, as it is they who have stood by me since those dark early days and provided me with all the support they could give.

But I am jumping the gun. All these wonderful things were still to happen for us, for, at this stage, we were not to know how on earth we would manage. Catherine just took hold of us all and we stepped off the cliff into the unknown ... because it was, quite simply, the only way to go.

It was a long, frustrating wait while the house was prepared for me, and the final stages of my nine-month rehabilitation inched towards their conclusion. After that, it would be the great unknown – life at home. Frankly, I could see very little point in being where I was now and longed to be allowed to go home. As for the future, I had no idea how I was going to cope with it, beyond a dogged determination to try and focus on one day at a time. Coping with the pain of what had happened was quite another thing and I was to discover what I suppose I had known all along, that being at home would never be able to remove that. Still, for now it would certainly alleviate the numbing ache of depression that accompanied my contemplation of the next six weeks of hospital life. After nearly a year, I had, quite honestly, had enough.

Our attention was distracted somewhat during this period by the search for a suitable vehicle, which would meet all my overall requirements, and which Catherine insisted we could not do without if home were not to become just another sort of prison. This was not an easy one to crack. Firstly, it would have to be roomy enough to take my enormous wheelchair, and have sufficient headroom to accommodate my height seated in the chair, and have been converted to take a wheel-chair passenger who could not transfer to a normal seat. Most German and British cars were excluded by the height requirements or because they were way too expensive, so we had to settle for a van, basically a converted goods vehicle or tradesman's van. The next problem, once we had actually found the right vehicle, after weeks of phoning and Internet searches, was the fact that we just couldn't afford it. We had decided to use what remained of the reserves, but that still left us with a shortfall of several thousands of pounds. Then an amazing thing happened. A friend decided to try and run a charity event to raise the money towards it.

She managed to get more than half of the shortfall together at one big event and my parents supplied the rest. A very close friend of ours with whom I go back a long way very kindly agreed to help with the negotiating side of the deal and with advice on the condition of the van, as Catherine had neither the knowledge nor the time to do so. He secured a great deal for us and also threw in a new winch as a present, which proved invaluable in getting me in and out of the thing.

We were not to know it, but this was to be the beginning of a fund-raising effort which was taken over by another very special friend when we were finally at home, and which has changed my life in every sense of the word. This, however, was only the beginning. Over the next few years, a number of fantastic friends and generous donors were to improve things for me in an amazing way, but I had not the slightest suspicion of any of this at this stage; nor, indeed, could I begin to guess how they would touch my life with such kindness and warmth later on. Still, when I contemplated the remaining time in hospital, it helped to know that the house alterations were progressing apace, and that I now had a vehicle too.

Confinement breeds contemplation. While waiting for Catherine to arrive or during the long night hours, I frequently contemplated other famous examples of incarceration. I imagined myself into their fate behind bars, or as we still say in German, behind 'Swedish curtains', a hangover from the days of the Thirty Years' War, which left many lasting scars.

As a boy growing up in Lower Saxony, I had often heard local country people talk of the times when Gustavus Adolphus, Wallenstein and Piccolomini slogged it out across the length and breadth of Germany, rampaging and destroying, leaving desolation in their wake. The ghostly image of the Swedish king riding on his white horse over the sky after his fatal final battle is still sung about some 350 years on. Stories are also still told to this day of a mysterious band of local men who withdrew into the forests and lived as partisans, hidden from the population and desperate to avoid capture. They called themselves the 'werewolves' and plenty of terrifying tales exist about their exploits. In fact, whole communities were forced into hiding.

Living like that, though, I reflected, was its own kind of imprisonment, since inevitably such a life meant the surrender of liberty in the wider sense. All partisans in subsequent generations have faced the same dilemma, the irony of choosing liberty in the form of an outlaw existence on the fringes of community, with a price on your head. I even saw the remnants of these communities once with my own eyes, when, back in the 1980s, while I was serving with the voluntary fire brigade, we went on a response call to a forest fire on the edge of a dried-out swamp. Extraordinary that isolated pockets of such communities can still exist in such an otherwise densely populated region.

Images of werewolves, but not in the modern horror movie sense of the word, thus populated my hours of darkness, and led me on to the mental puzzle of trying to reconstruct all kinds of stories I had read in childhood. This, obviously, was a rich fund of mental challenges for my nocturnal flights of the imagination, and kept me busy through many a difficult night, piecing together as much as I could remember of the novels I had read during my teens.

Another occupation I found myself indulging in during the

long hours when Catherine and the children weren't there was my game of 'guess who's walking along the corridor'. There was a multitude of signs to determine who was out there. One could rely on the occasional, rather specific laugh to pinpoint the individual; but they were few and far between, so a more dependable method had to be found. Some nurses walked on the front of their feet; and others, usually continent-specific, didn't lift their heels. The chewing of gum was widespread and must have been part of the job mandate. Most of the staff chewed away monotonously, like the revolving pistons of a low-revved engine. If two had stopped outside my door for a chat, I could usually tell by the sound waves emitted how far the mouth was left open and this was a particular giveaway. But the constant blowing and bursting of bubbles was a sure way of pinpointing the individual.

Nature abhors a vacuum, they say, and my brain was working overtime to fill mine.

The days drifted by endlessly like this and slowly, very slowly, I inched towards the door of release. This period was not without its own discoveries, however, and one of the nicest things I learned at this time came from a delightful Ugandan nurse who had been with me on this ward since I arrived. She had on many occasions tried to convince my daughters that it is a thing of beauty to swing your hips as you walk, regardless of their size. Whenever she saw them, she wasted no time in demonstrating what she meant. Apparently, where she came from it was also common practice to thank someone for their kindness by giving them a goat as a present. Something along the lines of 'say it with goats'. The children tried to persuade Catherine to turn up with a real baby goat tethered to a rope on my last day, but, mindful of the fact that there is not much pasture to be had in London, and that there were not many goats to be seen walking the streets with their mistresses, she settled for a plastic version instead. It still managed to raise hoots of joy and brought a few tears to her eyes.

When the day of my discharge arrived it was hard to believe that the time had finally come. Even harder to believe, though, that this was me. I would now have to return home to the impossible task of trying to reconnect with myself. How I was to do this seemed as daunting as it was painful, when my brain refused in the first place to recognise that this was now me. The big build-up to leaving was inevitably something of an anticlimax. As I was wheeled out of that building and into the waiting ambulance, however, I swore to myself that not for anything in the world would I ever accept returning to hospital again. Not for anything . . . well, on second thoughts, there would be one thing, but if I were granted that, I wouldn't need the hospital in the first place, would I?

Learning How to Live

It's the middle of the night. I lie in my bed near to Hasso, awake and alert, despite the overwhelming tiredness. Beyond the windows, black night has blotted out the garden and the village beyond. Without streetlamps here in the country, the moon only casts its light if the sky is cloudless. Inside, though, the room is never quite dark. Tiny red lights from Hasso's various pieces of hospital equipment glimmer in the darkened room, casting an eerie half-light. Nor is there ever any silence in the dead of night. The regulating pump for the air mattress occasionally breathes to adjust the pressure and the feeding apparatus attached to the tube in Hasso's stomach whirrs away. From time to time he sighs, long and low, on his outward breath.

It's hard to believe that after almost a year of hospital life, he is now home for good. Although I have had several weeks to get used to things, this new life still feels very strange. The level of responsibility, for one thing, is frequently a little daunting. For most hours of the day and all of the night, there are now no doctors or nurses at hand. Just Hasso and me, alone. Whatever problems arise, whether they be minor or serious, from now on I will have to deal with them on my own. And, should we actually need to summon a doctor, it will be the ordinary on-call GP service, and we will have to wait like anyone else. Otherwise, it's now up to me to manage Hasso's care, to administer his medication, keep the feeding regime going and cope with the unforeseen.

I can hear him breathing heavily in the bed near me. I know he's not asleep. He hardly ever manages to sleep for more than an hour or so at a time and sometimes lies awake on and off for most of the long night hours. Since the final removal of the trachi, his breathing is always loud and often laboured. He has to be propped up on several pillows to prevent him from choking and so is forced to spend each night almost sitting up. His arms and hands lie motionless at his side, attached to splints to prevent them shrinking and curling stiffly out of shape and worsening his pain. Attached to the thumb of his right hand splint is a tiny, sensitive switch. If he can manage to depress his thumb very slightly, the switch will activate an alarm so I can be made aware that he needs help. This could be for a myriad of reasons. He might be too cold or too hot. He could be in pain and need to be repositioned or he might simply have an itch he can't scratch. Before I can help him, he'll need to spell out with eye blinks exactly what's wrong. This can be agonisingly slow when the cause is something very uncomfortable.

Sometimes it's more serious. There's no way of knowing what each night will bring. As I lie there, listening to him breathing, following the muffled mechanical sounds, I can't help my brain wandering towards the dread fear that any night could be the abrupt beginning of a crisis and that he might not reach the morning. I try hard to block out this thought, to discipline my mind to banish it, but it's there every night, waiting silently for me in the long wakeful hours.

I can feel him staring into the dim shadows of the room; sense the thoughts shifting slowly within his brain. I try yet again, for the millionth time, to imagine what it must be like . . . and know I can't.

Instead, I resume my search for sleep. I'm so exhausted, but sleep is so elusive. I know I have to be able to rest. I know that I desperately need this sleep. Just for a short time, I tell myself, just for an hour or so till he needs me again. I know that without sleep I won't be able to keep up the pace, that I will start fraying at the edges and won't be able to carry on doing everything I need to do. I close my eyes and tell myself to relax. I can feel Hasso willing me towards the sleep that eludes him.

Click, whirr. The pump pushes another few drops of liquid feed into his stomach. The mattress creaks a little.

There are so many things to adjust to in this new life. Having spent so long away from home in the clinical environment of a hospital, Hasso probably hadn't realised how used to its structure and routine he had become. It's been a shock to discover that the familiar environment of the home he had longed for could feel so alien. The seductive power of habit has crept into his perception of things, despite his attempts to resist. And there are other fundamental changes that neither he nor I can get used to. The pain of our separation during the past year has been immense, but even now that he is home, we can't really be together as we once were. Even at night, now that he has to be propped up inside the barred sides of a hospital bed with tubes attached to various machines, the cold impossibility of sharing a bed is a deep and lasting source of distress. Together and yet not. Our new life is filled with such ironies.

The children also have a lot of adjusting to do now that he is home all the time. Yet it's amazing how love can provide the bridge across a sea of pain and loss. At first, they wanted to be round him all the time and weren't sure about how he was taking it, sensitive to his difficulties in adjusting. But, as time has gone on, they have evolved their own new version of our old family life. They have slipped into a kind of new normality, coming in to chat to him from time to time, sitting on the edge of his bed holding his hand while they watch TV together, telling him jokes and reading the eye blinks to hear his. And, strangely, unexpectedly, there is a deep and moving sort of comfort in all of this. It is what he has dreamed of for so long. The tiny, precious compensation that no one can now take away from him.

In practical terms, things are far from perfect. There is still so much that needs changing. For a start, the equipment isn't yet adequate, the care is still minimal and we need to arrange proper physiotherapy. Lying in the darkness, my brain teems with plans for improving things. I realise with a touch of cynicism that for the moment, practicalities seem to have become my new weapon against despair. Now I have had to assume so much more control than I have been allowed in a whole year, I am forced to manage the day-to-day with schemes and plans for Hasso's care. I fill my mind with essentials, with lists of tasks and jobs to do. It's a way, I know, of avoiding the stark reality of the future that surrounds us. I concentrate on just trying to be adequate, on getting it right. There is, after all, more than enough on this front to keep my mind busy. It's a ruse, I admit it. But I don't know any other way to cope. There's a problem with this, though, and I'm aware of it. The day must surely come when I will have provided him with all the material, practical aids and comforts imaginable and there will be literally nothing more I can do to ameliorate things. There will be no more plans to elaborate, no more equipment to find or therapists to enlist. Then I will have to face up to this blankness and understand how to go forward. In a word, to live. But not yet. For now my brain refuses to stop racing.

Hasso breathes a long protracted sigh. His eyes will be reaching into the dark corners of the room, running over the familiar shapes, remembering. In this room which used to be our living room, he has painted the walls himself, laid the wooden floor, fixed the oak cupboards to the walls and hung the doors. He has lit hundreds of fires in the grate and we have watched the dying embers together late into the night, long after the children have gone to bed, Hasso with his long legs stretched out beside mine on the floor, our faces warm, our hearts content. He has spent hours in this room, drinking wine as the summer sun dips through the windows and telling tall stories, or reading to the children on autumn evenings. Now the sofa has given way to his new bed and the armchairs have been replaced with his large mechanical hoist and huge wheelchair. New double doors have been put in the wall to give access to a small shower room where our utility room once was, and where a giant shower trolley is now parked with just inches to spare. It's not really as he had planned it when we first walked in here some years ago, saw the garden and said we'd buy the place. But it is the closest we can give him to the dreams he's had in hospital for nearly a year now.

The sigh peters out and his low, troubled breathing resumes.

In the still semi-darkness a great yearning overwhelms me. I feel the weight of all the memories and all the longing. There are words hanging in the silence and an immutable sense of belonging in the stillness. I slip out of bed and wrap a blanket round my shoulders to keep out the chill of the room. He is looking up at me through the glimmer, his eyes like the sea, the blue all dark and deep in the absence of light.

I lean in towards him and take his face in my hands. For a fragment of time, the knowledge that he is still here with me is, inexplicably, almost enough. I search the familiar corners of his face and look deep into the eyes that hold mine. There is such a sense of wonder in that feeling as he holds my gaze.

I reach down and close my hand around his, lifting the

palm away from the hard splint, tracing the shape of his fingers, feeling their warmth. I let my head sink down towards his onto the blank whiteness of the pillow. And for a moment, for a precious fleeting moment, we are at peace.

Facing the Future

By the time I was finally discharged from hospital, I had been away from home for a few days short of a year. I had left a memory of myself and my life behind me the year before, and was now returning to an existence which I could hardly recognise. It was time to try to be a family again. At the very least, it was time to give my children their mummy back.

What had changed within me then? Well, one of the greatest changes to me deep down is best described as feeling everything with a greater intensity. Where in the past I might have described myself on occasion as sad, for example, now I feel crushed with the weight of sadness and often dissolve into uncontrollable sobs, when I can no longer keep the lid on my pain. It is as if I feel an exaggeration of any emotional feeling. I know that other more minor cases of stroke often result in a serious alteration of personality, and that some victims even have the misfortune of finding themselves reduced to conversing in some sort of obscure dialect of a long forgotten language every time they open their mouths. If I were actually able to speak in my old voice, it would be obvious to everyone that, whatever terrible things may have happened to me, that isn't one of them. But the loss of speech did feel like yet 'another brick in the wall'. It still holds me captive and I have not learned to bear its pain and frustration to this day.

After the better part of a year spent in hospitals, I felt I was returning home after a lifetime. I had to remind myself that this was only a fraction of the twenty-eight summers Robinson Crusoe had to spend away from home, after he was ship-wrecked. But then Robinson Crusoe did finally find a way off his desert island, and leaving hospital, I knew with agonising clarity, was not the end of my ordeal, but merely the close of the first chapter.

My most earnestly felt desire has always been to be able, some day, to make my body respond to my brain. I hate having to lie on my back or sit in my wheelchair, forever like a helpless tortoise, welcoming visiting guests with a slight lifting of my right hand. This, needless to say, has never materialised. All there is on offer is a very limited half an armful of movement. My right hand has recovered a little movement in some fingers, but I still can't grip or lift anything enough to be able to make a difference to my huge level of dependence. Even this has only been possible, I tell myself, because my right arm really was the strongest part of me. This was due, in no small measure, to my passion for sawing up any suitable piece of wood in sight in order to feed my compulsions as a pyromaniac. This even went as far as Christmas trees, which only ever left our house after Epiphany through the chimney, in a kind of controlled, warm, demolition job.

The bottom line, however, is that all my hopes and desires hinge only on recovering something of myself and, to my intense sadness, this remains stubbornly beyond my grasp.

As for the rest of my thoughts, they are locked up now mostly in my memories, and in my dreams of what has been. I cannot attempt to describe these, as there is so much more to tell. Fragments of these dreams will have to suffice.

There is, for example, that arrow I made as a boy out of hazel wood and turkey feathers, which hangs above my computer as I write this. Each time I look at it, I am transported back to the joyous romps of my boyhood, to what felt then like endless summers, spent in the countryside around my home and also on the estate of an ageing aunt. The summer holidays I spent with her will remain with me forever, as will the stories she told me of her own youth. While staying with her, I also met the elderly mother of her sister-in-law, a Russian princess, born long before the peace accord of Brest-Litovsk in 1918 (which in the long run didn't bring much of a peace to Europe). I revelled in her reminiscences of her time as a young debutante, attending balls at the Imperial Court in St Petersburg, and of the glamour of the Tsar and his family. Strangely enough, during the winter of the year I came home from hospital, Catherine and I listened together to the talking book version of *Anna Karenina*, which so beautifully recreates the atmosphere of those times, and of life in nineteenth-century Russia. I had only to glance at my arrow to feel my connection with that world.

Indeed, not only was I connected in this way with Tsarist Russia, but this old lady was herself also linked to my family in another way. Her husband, a dragoon, had served in the very regiment that had been named after perhaps the most famous Bredow in the family, a general, who had commanded six squadrons of cavalry at the Battle of Mars-la-Tour in 1870. This battle has gone down in history as one of the most famous cavalry confrontations of all time. Indeed, I have been told that it is still taught as such at Sandhurst to this day. In an apparently near suicidal attack, Major General Friedrich Wilhelm Adalbert von Bredow led an uphill cavalry charge against dominant positions of opposing field horse artillery. This later became known as 'von Bredow's death ride'. But, against all odds, it succeeded and sealed the fate of the French. Germany's victory and subsequent growth of influence ultimately led to a change in Britain's position. This, in turn, helped to set the scene for the outbreak of war in 1914, a tragedy of immeasurable proportions, which pitched my countrymen against Catherine's and the rest of Europe in a struggle of obscene agonies, not for the only time in that century.

All this, and much more, was contained for me in that little arrow, which I had fashioned with such care in the woods so many years ago, and which now hangs on my wall. A silent witness to a time before the world went wrong.

So my time in hospital was up and, from now on, we were pretty much on our own. Virtually within days of coming home, though, pain in both upper thighs emerged and, as the sole person responsible for me at home, it was now up to Catherine to sort out problems such as these. In fact, this was the beginning of a new stage of the odyssey. We would have to develop new levels of self-reliance and would pursue several different avenues in our quest to realise my dreams, and also just to cope with my ever-increasing problems. This involved many new treatments, from botulinum injections, to electromagnetic mats, to harnessing cosmonaut technology for boosting the rate of healing, and several other weird and wonderful alternative therapies. Little has changed, but I have been told so many times to take a long-term view that I can only say that I try to keep an open mind.

Opening Door

There's an image that keeps coming back to me. I'm opening
a door and there in the sunshine I experience a small miracle.
It's a memory actually, a crystal-clear picture which is strangely
three-dimensional. It floats up into my consciousness at all
kinds of times and comes unbidden through the night hours,
even though I seem to be incapable of summoning it at will.
It's as if I keep tumbling, by accident, through a tiny gap in
time and finding myself back in that moment, because for an
instant it feels so very real. I can hear, see and even smell every
detail.

It's a warm summer's morning, early. Hasso has been away
on a business trip in Hong Kong and I am expecting him
home later that day. I hate those long separations when he's
away travelling for the bank. This time has been particularly
difficult to get through, not because of any reason in particular,
but because I have missed him so much. The weather has
been good; the children haven't had any problems. I've been
happy enough, but his absence for nearly three weeks has
gnawed away at me. I want him home.

There are several hours to go before his plane gets in, but
I'm awake early, listening to the birds and hoping all goes well
with the flight. The breeze coming in through the window is
already warm. From where I lie I can see the immense blue
of the sky and it's almost mesmerising to stare into its vastness.

I get up and shower. As I turn off the water, I think I can hear the front doorbell ringing. I hurriedly dry off and put on a bathrobe to go and check, but I'm pretty sure there's no one there because it's far too early. Unless it's the postman. I hurry down the stairs and see a shape through the frosted glass. Hasso?

I open the door and there he is. All of four hours early. Smiling and excited to have made it home long before he had dared to hope, his eyes all alive with pleasure. For a millisecond it happens, the miracle. Not having expected it to be him, my brain needs a fraction of an instant to catch up and in that moment it is as though I am seeing him for the first time all over again. I take in his laughing eyes, his skin, his height, his hair. It takes no more than that fraction of a second to show my joy and fall into his arms, but, in that tiny moment before, time has double-flipped and caught my heart in the shock of the new through the mystery of the familiar. It is a perfect alchemy of recognition and desire. A magical tap on the shoulder reminding me how my feelings for him run like an electric current beneath the mundane surface of the day to day. It is both surprising and wonderfully uplifting.

I love that moment. The joy in his eyes, the sun in his hair, the feel of his body beneath his shirt, the surprise of it all. He bear-hugs me and I feel his heart beating, the strength in his chest and arms. I smell the warm, moist morning air on the skin of his freshly shaven face. All that in the tiniest of split-second memories.

And then we go in and life takes over.

I really can't for the life of me remember what happened after that or what countless immemorable little events of normal domestic life followed on. But the immediacy of the shock and the intense pleasure of it have stayed with me ever since. And it keeps coming back, all the time. I can't *make* it return, it always stubbornly resists my voluntary attempts to summon it at will. But at completely random moments, there it is. I am opening the door and seeing him there again as if for the first time. Over and over.

There are thousands of memories teeming just below the surface. There always are with those we love. Time eats up so many of the moments we spend together and somehow it's awful how we lose them. They become faint vapours which float up and dissipate before we can hold them down. The millions of tiny events that make up a life together. Now, to me, each one seems so precious that my brain tries desperately to retrieve them, flailing about in an indistinct sea of memory, trying to recover the tiniest of moments. There are the old, well-beloved echoes and then the sharp, bright shards of joy that bring back long-lost moments we seem to have forgotten ever even living through. Others summon our attention with insistence and we concentrate all our will on the effort to recover them to some kind of vibrant, vital clarity. Like priceless pearls that we know are there, but which have sunk below the surface of the cloudy water and we fear have been lost for ever. But, try as I might to retrieve them from the sludge of my accumulated past and the most precious days of my memories, they are nebulous and slippery and, like stubborn children, will not be caught, tamed or caged.

That's what makes this memory so special. It arrives in my consciousness without warning and cannot be controlled. It is multi-layered and complete, down to the colour of Hasso's shirt and that cool damp smell on his skin. It is fleeting and brief, yet contains all of me and all of him. It is gone in the fraction of a second, but leaves me breathless and aching.

Each time it floods through my mind's eye I feel the briefest moment of trepidation as my hand reaches out to turn the handle of the door. For I know that on the other side of that door is everything I long for.

I'm terrified that one day the door will open and he will not be there.

Tomorrow

I have met many interesting and wonderful people since I came home from hospital. A strong, vibrant sense of togetherness and real community in our village has demonstrated what pulling together can actually achieve. Their response to my predicament has been just marvellous, but there is more to say. Old and new friends have contributed individually to a degree that has left me deeply moved, and the amazing results of all the fundraising have made all the difference to me. I have experienced so much kindness and genuine warmth and, although it is often the case that being close to such adversity brings out the best in people, it is certainly true to say that the affection and respect I have for all those who have helped me know no bounds.

Of course, one of the toughest things is that I really do miss the stimulation and challenge of work. My job was stressful and exhausting at times, but I enjoyed the professionalism and warmth of so many of my colleagues, especially the many laughs we had together. I must admit to having a peculiar habit of coming up with pretty outrageous ideas, something which the people at work were often responsible for firing up and encouraging. For example, I used to spend a lot of my spare time working out new practical jokes and this usually provoked quite a lot of amusement. Their favourite story about me was the crazy experiment I came up with for testing the strength of alcohol on pigeons. I discovered in my garden one day that grain soaked in Schnapps has a truly staggering effect and I loved to imagine the impact it would have on a place like Trafalgar Square, though I never got the chance to try that one out.

One thing is certain, though. Throughout my professional life, time always seemed to be in short supply. Now, inevitably, I often feel weighed down by so much of it that I can't fill. Often the clocks on the wall are just too blurred to my damaged eyes to make head or tail of them, so I usually find myself relying on the size of the shadows on the outside walls and the pools of light shifting round my room to make a guess at the time. With so much time on my hands, my memories have become so important to me.

Mostly, though, I miss the simple things. Life as it used to be with Catherine and the children. Just being together and having each other. Without them, of course, everything would be totally different. Not one day have I been left to rot away alone in this state, or to join the ranks of the sad, lonely victims of this cruel condition who have no one to be there for them. The stroke nurse in my second hospital had asked Catherine to get used to visiting me less, and to learn to re-engage with life a bit. This was repeated to her many times by different people along the way. Her answer came in the tens of thousands of miles on public transport and by car she clocked up every single day, without exception, while I was in hospital. She has replied to that request with the deter-mination she has shown not to leave me alone to my fate, but to transform our home into a kind of high-dependency ward, so I can at least live with those I love, and not be alone and desperate in a home somewhere. Little did she know, nearly twenty years ago, when, after knowing me for only three days, she let me make a date to ask her father formally for her hand, that she would end up looking after a disabled, constantly dribbling, but grateful husband. It truly has been a love story, and one that has lasted against all the odds.

The children, well, they are the future. Raising them as we had always done together is no longer possible, though, and that is really very hard for me. I could, of course, be a bit of a nag in the past. Remarks from me like, 'Elbows off the table!', 'Close your mouth while you're eating!' and so on, were an all-too-familiar sound to them. Now, even what I would normally say with my usual irony when I see someone dressed badly ('I wouldn't like anyone to see me hanging dead on a fence looking like that') has probably become just a distant memory. But quite the most unbearable thing of all is not being able to say out loud to them what is in my heart all the time, that I'm so proud of them and that I love them so fiercely. I can still tell them this, but the words have to be spelt out with eye blinks, and that, let's face it, can never be the same.

Looking at the whole scenario from where I am now, I would truly have appreciated knowing upfront that this kind of stroke is not necessarily a death sentence, but that it was never going to be life as I had known it. In spite of all my efforts, I seem no closer to that than I was on 1 May 2000. Living with that realisation is by far the hardest thing. Being the eternal optimist that I am, though, I still keep trying to drive it all upwards; nevertheless at times, the wholly random nature of 'upwards' feeling ever more like 'backwards' has a way of getting me down. Then come the dark moments and they are not somewhere I want to take you. I will never write about them, anyway, for there are no words to describe them.

Most of my time, however, is still filled with lots of waiting and time-killing, as well as trying out all manner of new ideas to get me back on track, which, to be honest, never seem to work. The rest is spent now within my own four walls with my loved ones around me. In spite of all Old Nick's determination to get me, however, it seems that my number isn't quite up yet. Close shave, though. Fate, for the moment at least, has blown a raspberry at the maggots who were busily tying on their bibs and sharpening their knives at the prospect. Nevertheless, I am certainly not out of the woods yet. Not by a long shot.

As for life, and the living of it, I can say in all honesty that I miss it intensely. With hope dangling like that elusive carrot in front of your nose, though, it is still sometimes the case that you can actually continue to laugh occasionally. Is this possible all the time? No, of course not.

But sometimes, just sometimes, I get a glimpse of a future that would eclipse the present, a kind of vision of hope, I suppose, but of a future far beyond our present and immediate grasp. All my life I have seen hard work prevailing and even harder work winning through. This time hard work alone seems to fall far short of what's required, and I realise that I'm going to need all the help I can get from the one whose voice famously came from the Burning Bush. Nevertheless, there is an image I first came across as a child, first expressed many centuries ago, supposedly by Martin Luther, and which has always meant a lot to me. Its eternal optimism still shines through and says it all for me ... 'Even if I knew that the world would end tomorrow, I would still plant an apple tree today.'

Someone in hospital once asked me if I was able to accept what has happened. Accepting is not really possible. Suffice it to say that in my dreams I can still walk and talk, no problem.

And no one can live without dreams.

Afterword

Hasso lived for a further three years at home in the house he had left on that beautiful spring day in May 2000. In spite of his determination and his will to recover, his struggle for life ended when, after having survived many serious infections, he finally succumbed to pneumonia.

Supported by wonderful carers and district nurses, together with a hugely kind and dedicated GP, we managed to free him from that hospital life and to get him back home with us, where he stayed right up until the end, when many others pressed for him to be readmitted. Gradually, we acquired a wonderful support team whose devotion and commitment to Hasso were second to none. The essential thing was to give him back a little of his own life, the comforting, relative privacy of his own home.

Our life together over those three years encompassed more than a lifetime of struggle, emotion and pain. In all those months, all those weeks, all those days since the onset of the stroke, things in essence had not altered very much. He was breathing independently, but with immense difficulty and discomfort. He had regained a little head movement and a tiny residual amount in his right thumb, hand and arm. He couldn't speak, eat, smile properly, move to touch us, cry out when in pain or do anything for himself. He found himself faced daily with the intense personal humiliations of the consequences of his condition. And he was forced to fall back on communicating, as he had done on day one, by blinking his eyes to spell out words, a process as frustrating and reductive for a great talker as any psychological torture you may care to invent. He remained paralysed, mute, 'locked in'; with no conceivable way out in sight.

For hours each day Hasso put himself through a punishing regime of physical training on a special exercise machine provided by a support fund which had been organised by a close friend, pushing his unresponsive body through the rigours of his own programme of therapy. He had regular visits from physios and went once a week to the outpatient physio department at the local hospital. The rest of the time he devoted himself for a whole year, day in, day out, to writing this book on his computer. This had been specially adapted to allow him to use a touch-sensitive switch with his right thumb to generate letters one by one onto the screen, thus allowing him to produce real text. It was a grindingly slow process, but by these means he was able to release his story as he wished to tell it. When the book was done, he used the computer to create messages and to write to his family and friends. Otherwise 'normal' conversation took the form of his blinking out messages to us, a method that several friends and relatives, and most notably his carers, also quickly managed to master, thus enabling him to re-establish some form of communication with those around him.

A very real difference, however, was made by the intense loyalty and affection shown by his friends. Those who remained true, even when others could not, came, and continued coming to see him. This, more than anything, helped to restore his sense of belief in himself. His realisation that his dearest friends refused to let his physical limitations cut him off from them did so much to alleviate his isolation. Remarkably, they also discovered that Hasso's sense of humour, though perhaps even more cynical now, was indeed intact; and I have been told several times that they would emerge from an hour or two in his company feeling they had gained so much more than they had given. No matter how bleakly depressed he might be feeling before they arrived, he would always respond to their jokes, spell out a few hard-hitting ones of his own and send them away with a smile on their faces, even though all this had to be done with eye blinks to convey every single letter of every word.

So how did he live the unliveable?

It is true to say that in a very real sense life had ended for him back in May 2000. Since that time, however, and right up until the end, Hasso had truly fought for life. He was no quitter. He knew, surely more acutely than anyone could, how unbearable his existence was. I never ceased to be amazed, though, how his determination and his sheer belief in life drove him ever onwards, yearning towards hope and locked into a refusal to be defeated. His spirit and determination in turns astounded, appalled and humbled me. For nearly four years he faced himself and would not give in.

That is not to say that Hasso didn't know despair. Quite the opposite. As the one who was closest to him, I can attest to the overwhelmingly remorseless pain and the black, bleak sense of panic that engulfed him on a daily basis. 'A man can't live like this,' he told me. And, again and again, 'I miss my life.'

Over time, of course, such a struggle is debilitating, and there were times, many times when he wished it could be over. But ever and again, from somewhere inside himself, he would resurrect the strength to fight on, would reassert his sense of self and force himself to re-engage in the struggle.

Somewhere between Christmas 2003 and the end of January 2004, however, a subtle change crept in.

In that time of stark winter frost and dark cold days, the bleak and sharp space between the years, something had changed. He began to experience increasing amounts of pain all through his body, resulting in huge discomfort and diminishing tolerance for the hours spent in his wheelchair. A new infection began raging through his system. He doggedly resisted its progress but its effects were debilitating in the extreme. He had fought off many infections since the stroke, but there was no denying that this was different. This time he seemed to realise that this was now, in fact, far bigger than himself and all his collective willpower to resist it. The process that would eventually close the circle and would slowly nudge open the door of Hasso's prison had silently and inexorably begun. 'Unless a miracle happens,' he told me with his typical gift for understatement, 'I think my number's up.'

And, of course, he was right. The struggle was shocking. I cursed and agonised over my inadequacy in the face of it. It was a slow and dreadful closing off of things. In the silent void that progressively swallowed us over those days, I saw him suffer and sensed him slipping further and further from me.

Now, in the brief moment between the before and the after, my light was going out. It suddenly seemed to me not like a whole life at all, but closer to a mere moment, a single heartbeat. I felt the intensity of all those years run like quicksilver through my fingers and lose itself in the whispered silence of a final breath.

Late at night on 23rd February 2004, in the house he had left so unwillingly on that beautiful spring day, Hasso died, as he had wished, with all of us around him.

It was twenty-one years since I came face to face with the young man who was to change my life forever. And I know now with absolute certainty that, even if I could have lived each and every one of those intervening years another twenty-one times over, it would never have been enough.